Also by Michael Finkel

True Story: Murder, Memoir, Mea Culpa

The Stranger in the Woods

The Stranger in the Woods

The Extraordinary Story of the Last True Hermit

Michael Finkel

Alfred A. Knopf   New York   2017

THIS IS A BORZOI BOOK PUBLISHED BY ALFRED A. KNOPF

Copyright © 2017 by Michael Finkel

All rights reserved. Published in the United States by Alfred A. Knopf, a division of Penguin Random House LLC, New York, and distributed in Canada by Random House of Canada, a division of Penguin Random House Limited, Toronto.

www.aaknopf.com

Knopf, Borzoi Books, and the colophon are registered trademarks of Penguin Random House LLC.

A portion of this work was adapted from "The Strange and Curious Tale of the Last True Hermit," originally published in *GQ* magazine (August 4, 2014).

Library of Congress Cataloging-in-Publication Data
Names: Finkel, Michael, author.
Title: The stranger in the woods : the extraordinary story of the last true hermit / by Michael Finkel.
Description: First edition. | New York : Alfred A. Knopf, 2017. | "This is a Borzoi book"—Title page verso.
Identifiers: LCCN 2016029910 (print) | LCCN 2016037679 (ebook) | ISBN 9781101875681 | ISBN 9781101875698 (ebook) | ISBN 9781524711092 (open market)
Subjects: LCSH: Knight, Christopher Thomas, 1965– | Hermits—Maine—Smithfield Region—Biography. | Recluses—Maine—Smithfield Region—Biography. | Thieves—Maine—Smithfield Region—Biography. | Smithfield Region (Me.)—Biography. | Survival—Case studies. | Solitude—Case studies.
Classification: LCC CT9991.K65 F56 2017 (print) | LCC CT991.K65 (ebook) | DDC 974.1/22043092 [B]—dc23
LC record available at https://lccn.loc.gov/2016029910

Jacket photograph by Alan Sirulnikoff / Millennium Images, U.K.
Jacket design by Kelly Blair
Maps by Kristine Ellingsen

Manufactured in the United States of America
Published March 8, 2017
Second Printing, March 2017

In memory of
Eileen Myrna Baker Finkel

How many things there are that I do not want.

—SOCRATES, CIRCA 425 B.C.

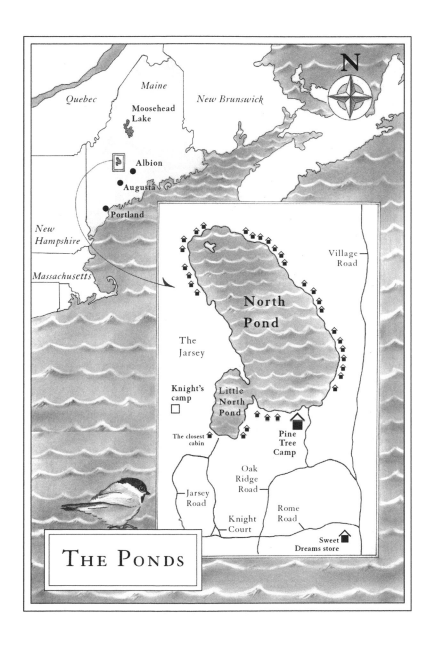

THE CAMP

The Stranger in the Woods

1
_____

The trees are mostly skinny where the hermit lives, but they're tangled over giant boulders with deadfall everywhere like pick-up sticks. There are no trails. Navigation, for nearly everyone, is a thrashing, branch-snapping ordeal, and at dark the place seems impenetrable.

This is when the hermit moves. He waits until midnight, shoulders his backpack and his bag of break-in tools, and sets out from camp. A penlight is clipped to a chain around his neck, but he doesn't need it yet. Every step is memorized.

He threads through the forest with precision and grace, twisting, striding, hardly a twig broken. On the ground there are still mounds of snow, sun-cupped and dirty, and slicks of mud—springtime, central Maine—but he avoids all of it. He bounds from rock to root to rock without a bootprint left behind.

One print, the hermit fears, might be enough to give him away. Secrecy is a fragile state, a single time undone and forever finished. A bootprint, if you're truly committed, is therefore not allowed, not once. Too risky. So he glides like a ghost between the hemlocks and maples and white birches and elms until he emerges at the rocky shoreline of a frozen pond.

It has a name, Little Pond, often called Little North Pond, though the hermit doesn't know it. He's stripped the world to his essentials, and proper names are not essential. He knows the season, intimately, its every gradation. He knows the moon, a sliver less than half tonight, waning. Typically, he'd await the new moon—darker is better—but his hunger had become critical. He knows the hour and minute. He's wearing an old windup watch to ensure that he budgets enough time to return before daybreak. He doesn't know, at least not without calculating, the year or the decade.

His intention is to cross the frozen water, but this plan is fast abandoned. The day had been relatively warm, a couple of ticks above freezing—the temperature he knows—and while he'd hunkered in his camp, the weather had worked against him. Solid ice is a gift to trackless stealth, but this touch of softness will emboss every footfall.

So the long way it is, back in the trees with the roots and the rocks. He knows the whole hopscotch for miles, all around Little North Pond and then to the farthest reaches of North Pond itself. He passes a dozen cabins, modest wood-sided vacation homes, unpainted, shut tight for the off-season. He's been inside many of them, but now is not the time. For nearly an hour he continues, still attempting to avoid footprints or broken branches. Some roots he's stepped on so often that they're worn smooth from repetition. Even knowing this, no tracker could ever find him.

He stops just before reaching his destination, the Pine

Tree summer camp. The camp isn't open, but maintenance has been around, and they've probably left some food in the kitchen, and there's likely leftovers from last season. From the shadow of the forest he observes the Pine Tree property, scanning the bunkhouses, the tool shop, the rec center, the dining hall. No one. A couple of cars are in the lot, as usual. Still, he waits. You can never be too cautious.

Eventually he's ready. Motion-detecting floodlights and cameras are scattered around the Pine Tree grounds, installed chiefly because of him, but these are a joke. Their boundaries are fixed—learn where they are and keep away. The hermit zigzags across the camp and stops at a specific rock, turns it over, grabs the key hidden beneath, and pockets it for later use. Then he climbs a slope to the parking lot and tests each vehicle's doors. A Ford pickup opens. He clicks on his penlight and peeks inside.

Candy! Always good. Ten rolls of Smarties, tossed in the cup holders. He stuffs them in another pocket. He also takes a rain poncho, unopened in its packaging, and a silver-colored Armitron analog watch. It's not an expensive watch—if it looks valuable, the hermit will not steal it. He has a moral code. But extra watches are important; when you live outside with rain and snow, breakage is inevitable.

He vectors past a few more motion cameras to a back door of the dining hall. Here he sets down his canvas gym bag of break-in tools and unzips it. Inside is a pair of putty knives, a paint scraper, a Leatherman multi-tool, several long-necked flathead screwdrivers, and three backup flashlights, among other items. He knows this door—it's already slightly scraped and dented from his work—and he selects a screwdriver and slots it into the gap between the door and frame, near the knob. One expert twist and the door pops open, and he slips inside.

Penlight on, clamped in his mouth. He's in the large camp kitchen, light flashing over stainless steel, a ceiling rack of sleeping ladles. Right turn, five paces, and to the pantry. He removes his backpack and scans the metal shelves. He grabs two tubs of coffee and drops them into his pack. Also some tortellini, a bag of marshmallows, a breakfast bar, and a pack of Humpty Dumpty potato chips.

What he really desires is at the other end of the kitchen, and he heads there now, takes out the key he'd collected from beneath the rock, and inserts it into the handle of the walk-in freezer. The key is attached to a plastic four-leaf-clover key chain with one of the leaves partially broken off. A three-and-a-half-leaf clover, perhaps still lucky yet. The handle turns and he enters the freezer, and the evening's entire mission, all the meticulous effort, feels immediately rewarded.

He is deeply, almost dangerously hungry. Back at his tent, his edible supplies are a couple of crackers, some ground coffee, and a few packets of artificial sweetener. That's it. If he'd waited much longer, he would have risked becoming tentbound from weakness. He shines his light on boxes of hamburger patties and blocks of cheese, bags of sausage and packs of bacon. His heart leaps and his stomach calls and he sets upon the food, loading it into his backpack; smorgasbord.

2

Terry Hughes's wife nudges him awake and he hears the beeps and he's out of bed like a spring uncoiled, game on. Quick check of the monitor then a dash down the stairs, where everything's in place: gun, flashlight, cell phone, handcuffs, sneakers. Duty belt. Duty belt? No time, forget the belt, now jump in the truck and head off.

A right onto Oak Ridge, then left in a half mile, accelerating down the long driveway to the Pine Tree Camp. Headlights are off but the truck's still noisy, so he throws it in park and vaults out of the cab. He continues on foot, fast as he can though less agile than usual. The lack of a belt means his hands are encumbered with gear.

Even so, it's full speed toward the dining hall, hurdling boulders, dodging trees, then a crouching scuttle to an exterior window. Heart pulsing like a hummingbird's; from his bed to the window in four minutes flat.

Hughes takes a breath. Then he cautiously lifts his head and steals a peek through the window, straining his eyes against the dimness of the Pine Tree kitchen. And he sees it: a person carrying a flashlight, the pale beam emanating from the open door of the walk-in freezer. Could this really, after all these years, be him? It must be. Hughes is still in his pajama pants, and he pats the clip-on holster on his waistband to make sure—yes, his weapon's there, a little Glock .357 Sig. Loaded. No safety switch.

The beam brightens and Hughes tenses and out of the freezer steps a man, hauling a backpack. He's not quite what Hughes expected. The man is bigger, for one thing, and cleaner, his face freshly shaved. He's wearing large nerdy eyeglasses and a wool ski cap; he roams the kitchen, seemingly unconcerned, selecting items as if in a grocery store.

Hughes permits himself a flicker of satisfaction. There are rare perfect moments in law enforcement, as Sergeant Hughes well knows. He's been a Maine game warden for eighteen years, and before that, for nearly a decade, he was a U.S. Marine. You might as well award him a PhD in grunt work, dead ends, and paper filing. But once in a beautiful while, wisdom gained through frustration pays dividends.

A few weeks previous, Hughes had resolved to end the reign of the hermit. He knew that none of the usual police methods were likely to work. After a quarter century of intermittent investigations, including foot searches, flyovers, and fingerprint dusting, conducted by four separate law enforcement agencies—two county sheriff's departments, the state police, and the game warden service—no one had even figured out the hermit's name. So Hughes questioned experts in high-tech surveillance, he brainstormed with private detectives, he spitballed ideas with friends from the military. Nothing they came up with felt right.

He phoned some acquaintances working border patrol up at Rangeley, near the Maine-Quebec crossing. It turned out that one of the guys had just returned from a training camp in which new Homeland Security equipment had been introduced—devices that offered a better method of tracking people who tried to sneak across borders. This was closely guarded technology, Hughes was told, far too sophisticated for anything a game warden might need. It sounded ideal. Hughes vowed to keep quiet about the specifics, and soon three border patrol agents were tromping around the Pine Tree kitchen.

They hid one sensor behind the ice machine, another on the juice dispenser. The data-receiving unit was installed in Hughes's home, at the top of the stairs, so that the alarm beeps would be audible in every room. Hughes devoted himself to learning the system until operating the device felt intuitive.

This was not enough. To trap the hermit, he could afford little margin for sloppiness. An errant noise while Hughes approached, an inadvertent glint from his flashlight, and his plan would probably fail. He memorized the motion lights, located the best spot to ditch his truck, and rehearsed every move from his house to the camp, shaving off seconds with each practice run. He made it a nightly habit to set out all his gear; the duty-belt oversight only proved he was human. Then he waited. It took two weeks. The beeps—first heard by his wife, Kim—came shortly after one o'clock in the morning.

All that, plus luck, for this perfect law enforcement moment. Hughes spies through the window as the burglar methodically fills his pack. No gray areas here; no circumstantial evidence. He has him dead to rights. And at the Pine Tree

Camp, no less. Pine Tree caters to children and adults with physical and developmental disabilities—it's a nonprofit organization, run off donations. Hughes is a longtime volunteer. He sometimes fishes with the campers on North Pond, catching bass and white perch. What kind of a guy breaks into a summer camp for disabled people, over and over?

Hughes eases away from the building, keeping his head low, and quietly makes a cell-phone call. Game wardens don't typically work burglary cases—usually it's more illegal hunters or lost hikers—and this effort has been chiefly a spare-time obsession. He asks the dispatch office of the Maine State Police to alert Trooper Diane Vance, who has also been chasing the hermit. They've been colleagues forever, Hughes and Vance, both graduating from their respective academies the same year, then working together on and off for nearly two decades. His idea is to let Vance handle the arrest. And the paperwork. He returns to the window to keep guard.

As Hughes watches, the man cinches his pack and heaves it to his shoulders. He departs the kitchen and disappears from Hughes's view, into the vast empty dining room. He's moving toward an exit, Hughes surmises, a different one from the door he'd pried open. Instinctively, Hughes maneuvers around the building to the spot where the man seems to be headed. This exterior door, like all the ones to the Pine Tree dining hall, is painted cherry red, trimmed with a green wooden frame. Hughes is without help, deep in the night, seconds away from a potentially violent encounter. It's a complicated instant, a fraught decision.

He is as prepared as possible for whatever might happen,

fistfight to shoot-out. Hughes is forty-four years old but still as strong as a rookie, with a jarhead haircut and a paper-crease jawline. He teaches hand-to-hand defensive tactics at the Maine Criminal Justice Academy. No way he's going to step aside and let the intruder go. The opportunity to disrupt a felony in progress overrides all concerns.

The burglar, Hughes thinks, is probably a military vet, and therefore likely armed. Maybe this guy's combat ability is as good as his forest skills. Hughes holds his position by the cherry-red door, Glock in his right hand, flashlight in his left, his back against the building's wall. He waits, running the contingencies through his mind, until he hears a small *clink* and sees the door handle turning.

The burglar steps out of the dining hall and Hughes flips on his Maglite, blazing it directly in the man's eyes, and trains the .357 square in the center of his nose, steadying his gun hand atop his flashlight hand, both arms extended. The two men are maybe a body's length apart, so Hughes hops back a few feet—he doesn't want the guy lunging at him—while ferociously bellowing a single phrase: "Get on the ground! Get on the ground! Get on the ground!"

3

As Diane Vance drives through the dark toward the Pine Tree Camp, all she knows is that Terry Hughes is in a risky situation, without backup, pursuing a man with an amazing ability to disappear. She's pretty certain that by the time she gets there, the guy will be gone. Or worse. He could have a gun; he could use it. This is why she's wearing a bulletproof vest. Hughes, she's aware, is not.

Vance drives past the forest-green Maine Warden Service truck stashed beside the Pine Tree driveway and heads directly to the dining hall. There's no sign of anyone. She steps from her squad car, wary, and calls out, "Sergeant Hughes? Sergeant Hughes?"

"I'm ten forty-six!" comes his response—Maine State Police code for suspect in custody—and Vance's concern promptly eases. Around a corner of the building she sees a scattered mess of food and a man lying on his stomach, arms behind his back. Upon being confronted by Hughes, the thief, stunned, had dropped to the cold cement without resistance. Only he's not completely in custody. The man is wearing a thick winter jacket, and the sleeves are interfering with Hughes's attempts to secure the handcuffs. Vance swoops in and restrains the suspect with her own set of cuffs, and now he's fully ten forty-six.

The officers guide the man into a sitting position, then help him to his feet. They pull everything out of his pockets—a pile of Smarties, the Armitron watch, the clover key chain—and check his backpack and gym bag for weapons. He could be a bomber, a terrorist, a murderer; the officers have no idea. They find only a Leatherman. The tool is engraved, commemorating the Pine Tree Camp overnight of 2000, thirteen years earlier.

The man is obeying the officers' commands but is not answering questions. He avoids eye contact. During their patdown and search, the officers were unable to locate any identification. He did have a wallet on him, camo-patterned with a velcro closure, but inside is only a sheaf of cash. The money is clearly very old, some of it moldy.

It's late, two a.m., but Hughes phones the Pine Tree Camp's facilities director, Harvey Chesley, who says he'll be on his way. Hughes has a master key that allows him access to the dining hall—Chesley had given it to him, with his blessing; anything to catch the hermit—and he unlocks a door, flips on the lights, and he and Vance escort the suspect back inside the place he just burglarized.

The dining room is cavernous and echoey, an expanse of blue linoleum beneath a vaulted ceiling of immense spruce rafters. It's the off-season, and all the tables and chairs are stacked against the walls. There is a row of windows on the pond side of the hall, but there's nothing to see in the dark.

Hughes and Vance drag a metal-framed chair with a maroon plastic seat into the center of the room, and they sit the suspect down, hands still locked behind his back.

The officers slide a folding table in front of him, then Vance also sits down, while Hughes remains standing. The man is still not speaking. The expression on his face appears blank and calm. It's unsettling; a person who has just been arrested after a sudden encounter should not be silent and impassive. Hughes wonders if he's insane.

The man is wearing new-looking blue jeans, a hooded gray sweatshirt beneath a nice Columbia jacket, and sturdy work boots. It's like he has just gone shopping at the mall. His backpack is from L. L. Bean. Only his eyeglasses, with chunky plastic frames, seem outdated. There's no dirt on him anywhere, and little more than a shading of stubble on his chin. He has no noticeable body odor. His thinning hair, mostly covered by his wool cap, is neatly cropped. His skin is strangely pale, with several scabs on his wrists. He's a little over six feet tall and broad-shouldered, maybe one hundred and eighty pounds.

Vance, like many officers who've searched for the hermit, always suspected that most of the story was mythical. Now she feels more certain. No way did this guy emerge from the woods. He has a home somewhere, or a hotel room, and was just coming around to burglarize places.

The camp facilities director, Chesley, soon arrives, as do the camp's maintenance man and, later, another game warden. Chesley immediately identifies the watch the officers had removed from the suspect's pocket. It belongs to his son, Alex, who'd left it in his truck, parked in the Pine Tree lot. The timepiece was not valuable but did have sentimental meaning; it had been a gift to Alex from his grandfather. The watch on the suspect's wrist, meanwhile, is claimed by the maintenance man, Steve Treadwell—it had been given to him by the Sappi Fine Paper Company, marking his twenty-fifth year of working at the Skowhegan plant.

There's a lot of commotion in the room, and the suspect's composure starts to fade. He remains seated and quiet but is soon visibly suffering, his arms shaking. Then Hughes has an idea. His confrontation with the man had been threatening and traumatic, but perhaps Vance can create a calmer atmosphere. Hughes herds all the men through a swinging door into the kitchen, leaving Vance alone with the suspect.

For a little while, she lets the air in the dining hall settle. She's followed this case, intrigued and bemused, for the entirety of her eighteen years on the force. She switches the handcuffs so the man's arms are in front and he can sit more comfortably. Hughes comes out with bottles of water and a plate of cookies, then retreats to the kitchen. Vance removes the handcuffs completely. The man takes a drink. He's been in custody for more than an hour and a half. Perhaps he's realized there will be no disappearing this time. Calmly, evenly, Vance reads him his rights. He has the right to remain silent. She asks for his name.

"My name is Christopher Thomas Knight," says the hermit.

4

"Date of birth?"

"December 7, 1965." The sounds passing through his mouth are stuttery and clanky, an old engine struggling to turn over, each syllable a chore. But at least it seems he's being understood; Vance is jotting things down.

"Age?"

The man is quiet again. His name and his birthday are durable relics, lodged in his brain. Much as you'd like, you apparently can't forget everything. Years, he's proven, are disposable. So he starts doing the math, uncurling his fingers to keep track. Okay, but what year is it now? They solve the problem together, he and Vance. It's 2013. Thursday, April 4. Christopher Knight is forty-seven years old.

"Address?" asks Vance.

"None," answers Knight.

"Where is your mail sent?"

"No mail."

"What address do you put on your tax return?"

"No tax returns."

"Where are your disability checks sent?"

"No checks."

"Where is your vehicle?"

"No vehicle."

"Who do you live with?"

"No one."

"Where do you live?"

"The woods."

This is not the appropriate time, Vance understands, to initiate a debate about the veracity of these claims. Best to let the man continue. "How long," she asks, "have you been living in the woods?"

"Decades," he says.

Vance would prefer something more specific. "Since what year?" she presses.

Once more with the years. He has made the decision to talk, and it's important to him to speak strictly the truth. Anything else would be wasting words. He concentrates for a time, gazing toward the windows, still black. He remembers something.

"What year," he asks, "was the Chernobyl nuclear-plant disaster?"

As soon as he says it, he wishes he hadn't. The police officer is going to think he's some lunatic environmental activist. It's really just a news event he happened to recall. But assembling all the language needed to clarify this seems impossible, so he lets it go. Vance thumbs her phone: Chernobyl was in 1986.

"That's when I took to the woods," says Knight. Twenty-seven years ago. He was not long out of high school, and now he's a middle-aged man. He says he passed the time living in a tent.

"Where?" asks Vance.

"Somewhere in the woods a distance away," says Knight. He never learned the name of his backyard pond, so naturally he doesn't know what township he's in: Rome, Maine; population one thousand and ten. He can, however, recite the name of every species of tree in his patch of forest, and in many cases describe the particular pattern of branches on those trees.

"Where did you stay during winter?" Vance asks.

He remained in his small nylon tent, he insists, and did not once in all those winters light a fire. Smoke might give his campsite away. Each autumn, he says, he stockpiled food at his camp, then didn't leave for five or six months, until the snow had melted enough for him to walk through the forest without leaving prints.

Vance needs a moment to consider this. Winters in Maine are long and intensely cold—a wet, windy cold, the worst kind of cold. A week of winter camping is impressive. An entire season is practically unheard of. She excuses herself and heads through the swinging door to the kitchen.

The men are drinking coffee, keeping watch on Knight through the large rectangular window in the door. Vance fills them in on what he said. No one is quite sure how much to believe. It's important, Hughes notes, before the man stops talking, to learn what he has to say about the break-in.

Vance returns to Knight, and Hughes, curious, props opens the door a little to hear. Virtually all criminals, he knows, will dispute any wrongdoing—they'll swear to God they didn't do it, even if you've just watched them do it.

"Do you want to tell me," Vance says to Knight, "how you got into this building?"

"I pried open a door with a screwdriver," says Knight. To enter the freezer, he adds, he used a key he'd stolen several seasons before. He points to the three-and-a-half-leaf-clover key chain among the items strewn on the table in front of him.

"Where did the money come from?" asks Vance, referring to the stack of cash, a total of $395, she'd removed from his wallet.

"I gathered it over the years," says Knight. A few bills here and there, mostly singles, from various places he broke into. He thought there might come a point when he'd have to walk into town to purchase something, but that did not happen. He says he spent no money the entire time he lived in the woods.

Vance asks Knight to estimate how many times he burglarized cabins or houses or camps. There's a protracted silence while Knight seems to be calculating. "Forty times a year," he eventually says. Over each of the last twenty-seven years.

Now it is Vance's turn to do the math. The total's more than a thousand—one thousand and eighty, to be exact. Each of them felonies. It's almost certainly the biggest burglary case in the history of Maine. Possibly, in terms of the number of separate break-ins, the largest in the country. Maybe the world.

Knight explains that he entered places strictly at night, after carefully trying to ensure that nobody was home. He never stole from anyone's full-time residence, where it was more likely someone could unexpectedly show up. Instead, he burglarized only summer cabins and the Pine Tree Camp. Sometimes the cabins were unlocked; sometimes he jimmied a window or forced open a door. Pine Tree alone he broke into perhaps a hundred times. He always took all he could carry, but it wasn't a lot, so he had to keep coming back.

Vance explains that he will have to forfeit all the stolen material he possesses. She asks Knight to claim what is his. "Everything is stolen," he says. His backpack, his boots, his break-in tools, the entirety of his campsite, and all the clothes he is wearing, right down to his underwear. "The only thing I can honestly say is mine," he states, "are my eyeglasses."

Vance asks if he has any family in the area. "I would rather not answer that," he says. He doesn't know if his parents are alive or dead—he has not been in contact with anyone—but if they are alive, he hopes they never learn that he's been found. Vance asks why, and Knight says that he wasn't raised to be a thief. He says that he is ashamed.

Knight does admit that he grew up in central Maine. He was never in the military. He says that he graduated from Lawrence High School, class of 1984. The Pine Tree Camp facilities director, Chesley, mentions that his wife also went to Lawrence, in the nearby town of Fairfield, graduating two years later. They might still have the 1984 yearbook at their house. Hughes asks Chesley to drive home and try to find it.

Vance calls dispatch and runs a check on Knight. He has no criminal record; there are no warrants for his arrest. He is not listed as a missing person. His driver's license expired on his birthday in 1987.

Chesley comes back with the yearbook, the *Lawrence Lyre,* its navy blue cover stamped with a big silver "84." The senior picture for Chris Knight, as he's called, shows a kid with dark tousled hair and thick-framed eyeglasses, arms crossed, leaning back slightly against a tree, wearing a blue polo shirt with two breast pockets. He looks healthy and strong. There's less a smile than a wry sort of smirk. He's not pictured with any sports team or school club or anywhere else.

It's hard to tell if the same person is now sitting in the Pine Tree dining hall. Knight says that he hasn't seen an image of himself in years, except maybe a blurry reflection in the water. There's no mirror at his campsite, he mentions.

"How do you shave?" asks Vance.

"Without a mirror," he says. He no longer knows what he looks like. He stares at the photo, squinting. His eyeglasses have been pushed up on his forehead, but now he moves them back to his nose.

And this is the moment, both Hughes and Vance agree, when they suddenly feel certain—they just sense in their guts—that everything they've heard tonight is true. The color of the frames may have faded over the decades, but the boy in the photo and the man in the dining hall are wearing similar pairs of glasses.

It's not long before dawn now; the darkness has crested. Knight, as Vance knows, will soon be swallowed by the legal system, and perhaps never speak freely again. She'd like an explanation—why leave the rest of the world behind?—but Knight says he can't give her a definitive reason.

She points to the scabs on his wrists. "What did you do for medicine?" she asks. "Or doctors?"

"I took no medications and never went to a doctor," says Knight. As he grew older, he says, cuts and bruises healed more slowly, but he did not once suffer a serious injury.

"Have you ever been sick?" asks Vance.

"No," says Knight. "You need to have contact with other humans to get sick."

"When is the last time you had contact with another human?"

He never had physical contact, Knight answers, but sometime in the 1990s, he encountered a hiker while walking in the woods.

"What did you say?" asks Vance.

"I said, 'Hi,'" Knight replies. Other than that single syllable, he insists, he had not spoken with or touched another human being, until this evening, for twenty-seven years.

5

Flashlights, for some families, were the first items to vanish. For others, it was a spare propane tank. Or books on a bedside table, or steaks you'd put in the freezer. In one cabin it was a cast-iron frying pan, a paring knife, and a coffeepot. Batteries, for sure, were missing—often every battery in the house.

It wasn't funny enough to be a joke, and it wasn't serious enough to be a crime. It occupied some unsettling place between. Maybe your kids took the flashlights. You *did* put those steaks in the freezer, didn't you? After all, your TV was still there, as was your computer, your camera, your stereo, and your jewelry. No windows or doors were broken. Do you call the police and tell them there's been a burglary, that all your D batteries and your Stephen King novel are gone? You do not.

But then you return to your cabin the following spring and the front door is unlocked. Or the dead bolt is undone. Or, in one case, the hot-water knob on the kitchen sink breaks off in your hand—easily, as though it has just been balanced there—and you examine the sink, then the window over the sink, and you see on the sill a few tiny white curls that look like file shavings. Then you notice that the metal lock on the window is open, and that the frame around the lock has been slightly scraped away.

Holy crap, someone has been inside—and probably stepped on your faucet while wriggling through the window, then made it look like nothing was broken. Again no valuables are missing, but this time you do call the police.

The police say they already know about the hermit and hope to have the case quickly solved. All summer, at barbecues and campfires, you hear a dozen similar tales. Propane tanks, batteries, and books are the constants, but also lost are an outdoor thermometer, a garden hose, a snow shovel, and a case of Heineken beer.

One couple opened their place for the season and discovered that there was no mattress on one of the bunk beds. This was baffling. You couldn't push a mattress out any of the cabin's windows, not even close. But the front door, the only door, had been bolted and padlocked for winter. The door had been sealed when they'd arrived, the lock untouched; there was no damage anywhere. The kitchen window, however, had been jimmied open. The only idea that made even a sliver of sense was that the thief came in through the window, pried the pins out of the front door's hinges, forced the door open from the hinge side, slid the mattress out, put the door back together, then exited through the window.

It was the Pine Tree Camp, everyone learned, that was the primary target, the thief's own private Costco. In every break-in, the damage was minimal—no broken glass, no ransacking. He was a thief, not a vandal. If he removed a door, he took the time to reattach it. Expensive items didn't seem to interest him. Or her. Or them. Nobody knew. Because of the type of articles that were stolen, one family called him the Mountain Man, but that frightened their children, so they changed it to the Hungry Man. Most people, including the police, began referring the intruder simply as the hermit, or the North Pond hermit, or, more formally, the hermit of North Pond. Some police reports mentioned "the legend of the hermit," and on others, where a suspect's full name was requested, he was recorded as Hermit Hermit.

Many North Pond residents were convinced that the hermit was actually a neighbor. North and Little North Ponds are in central Maine, away from the summer-congested coast and its moneyed enclaves. The roads that twist along their shorelines are mostly unpaved and bumpy, with about three hundred cabins scattered around the roughly twelve-mile circumference of the two ponds, the majority occupied only in warm weather. A few of the cabins still don't have electricity. Neighbors tend to know one another; there's not a lot of turnover. Some families have owned the same plot for a century.

Maybe, people speculated, the break-ins were carried out by a group of local teens—a gang initiation, a prank. Or, some locals guessed, it could have been the work of an antisocial Vietnam vet. More likely, others thought, it was an inside job at Pine Tree. There were also these suspicious-looking deer hunters who came from out of state. It might've been one of those airplane hijackers from the 1970s, still on the run. Possibly a serial killer. And what about that guy who was always fishing by himself—had anybody been inside his cabin? Perhaps you'd find your mattress there.

One summer, a family had an idea. They taped a pen on a string to their front door along with a handwritten note: "Please don't break in. Tell me what you need and I'll leave it out for you." This sparked a small fad, and soon a half dozen cabins had notes fluttering from their doors. Other residents hung shopping bags of books on their doorknobs, like donations to a school fund-raiser.

There was no reply to the notes; none of the shopping bags were touched. The break-ins continued: a sleeping bag, an insulated snowmobile suit, a year's worth of *National Geographic* magazines. Batteries and more batteries, including the blocky ones from cars and boats and ATVs. The same couple who lost their mattress had a backpack stolen, which triggered a panic—that was where they'd hidden their passports. Then they saw that the burglar had removed the passports and placed them in a closet before departing with the pack.

Many families eventually decided to reinforce their cabins. They installed alarm systems, motion lights, stronger windows, sturdier doors. Some spent thousands of dollars. A new phrase joined the lexicon of the lakes—"hermit-proofing"— and an unfamiliar tinge of distrust settled over the community. Families that never locked their doors began locking them. Two cousins, who own nearby cabins, each thought the other was taking his propane. Several people blamed themselves for constantly misplacing items and half-jokingly worried that they were beginning to lose their minds. One man suspected his own son of burglary.

The mattress-and-backpack couple decided that every time they left their cabin, even for an hour, they had to latch all the windows and set the bolt, no matter how stuffy it got inside. At the end of summer, one man returned from the hardware store with fifty sheets of plywood and a Makita screw gun, and used every one of his thousand screws to entomb his cabin for winter.

The thousand screws worked, but nothing else did. Gone from other cabins were pillows and blankets, toilet paper and coffee filters, plastic coolers and Game Boys. Some families were burglarized so frequently that they learned the hermit's tastes: peanut butter rather than tuna fish, Bud over Bud Light, briefs not boxers. He had a major sweet tooth. One kid lost all his Halloween candy; the Pine Tree Camp was short an industrial-sized tub of fudge.

Early in the lake season, before Memorial Day, there was usually a rash of break-ins, then another flurry late, after Labor Day. Otherwise it was always midweek, particularly on a rainy night. None of the full-time residents ever seemed to be victimized, and he didn't steal food items that had already been opened. One family had a running joke—"He won't date the skinny girl"—because no matter how many times their liquor cabinet was raided, he never touched the Skinny-girl margarita drink.

Ten years passed. It was the same story: almost no one could stop him, and the police couldn't catch him. He seemed to haunt the forest. Families returned from a quick trip into town wondering if they were going to encounter a burglar. They feared he was waiting in the woods, watching. He searched your cupboards and rummaged through your drawers. Every walk to the woodpile provoked a goose-bumpy feeling that someone was lurking behind a tree. All the normal night sounds became the noises of an intruder. A few friends quietly discussed putting rat poison in food and leaving bear traps in the leaves, though they never went through with these ideas.

Others said it was obvious that the hermit was harmless—just let him have your spatula and milk crates. He was hardly more trouble than the seasonal houseflies. Maine has always been a quirky place, stocked with odd characters, and now North Pond had its own folklore of a mysterious hermit. At least two kids wrote school papers about the legend.

But then the crimes became more brazen. One family loaded frozen chickens in a freezer for a party and lost them all at once. At a North Pond home owners' meeting in 2004, nearly fifteen years into the mystery, the hundred people present were asked who had suffered break-ins. At least seventy-five raised their hands.

Then, at last, there was seemingly a breakthrough. As the price and size of motion-sensing security cameras decreased, several families installed them. At one cabin, where the camera was hidden in a smoke detector, there was success: the hermit was captured on film, peering into a refrigerator. The images were confusing. The thief's face wasn't in focus, but they appeared to show a clean, well-dressed man who was neither emaciated nor bearded—highly unlikely to have been roughing it in the woods. He didn't appear nimble, or strong, or even outdoorsy. "Mr. Ordinary," one person called him. It was probable, people deduced, that this so-called hermit had been a neighbor all along.

No matter. With these first photos, and then others, the police were confident that capture was imminent. The images were hung in shops, post offices, town halls. A couple of officers went from cabin to cabin. Maddeningly, nobody could identify the man pictured, and the burglaries continued.

Another decade elapsed. The break-ins at Pine Tree increased in both frequency and quantity of goods stolen. By this point, a quarter century in, the whole thing was absurd. There was the Loch Ness monster, the Himalayan yeti, and the North Pond hermit. One man, desperate for an answer, spent fourteen nights over the course of two summers hiding in his cabin, in the dark, holding a .357 Magnum and waiting for the hermit to break in. No luck.

The general consensus was that the original thief must be retired or dead and the latest break-ins were copycat crimes. Maybe there was a second generation of that teenage gang, or a third. Kids who'd grown up with the hermit now had kids of their own. Most people resigned themselves to the idea that this was the way it would be; you'd just replace your boat battery and propane tank each summer, and go about your life. The couple who'd lost the backpack and mattress was now missing a new pair of Lands' End blue jeans—thirty-eight-inch waist, with a brown leather belt.

Finally, the most unexpected thing of all happened. The Loch Ness monster didn't emerge from the lake; the yeti wasn't caught strolling around Mount Everest. There are no little green men from Mars. But the North Pond hermit, it turns out, was real. When he was captured by Sergeant Hughes, he was wearing Lands' End jeans, size thirty-eight, cinched with a brown leather belt.

6

Christopher Knight was arrested, charged with burglary and theft, and transported to the Kennebec County Correctional Facility, in the state capital of Augusta. For the first time in nearly ten thousand nights, he slept indoors.

The *Kennebec Journal* broke the story, and the news elicited some strong and curious reactions. The jail was inundated with letters and phone calls and visitors; "a circus," Chief Deputy Sheriff Ryan Reardon called it. A carpenter from Georgia volunteered to repair any cabin Knight had damaged. A woman wanted to propose marriage. One person offered Knight land to live on, rent-free, while another pledged a room in his house.

People sent checks and cash. A poet sought biographical details. According to Chief Deputy Sheriff Reardon, two men, one from New York and another from New Hampshire, arrived at the jail with $5,000 in cash, Knight's total bail. Knight was soon deemed a flight risk, and his bail was raised to $250,000.

Five songs were recorded: "We Don't Know the North Pond Hermit," "The Hermit of North Pond," "The North Pond Hermit," "A Hermit's Voice," and "North Pond

Hermit"—bluegrass, folk, alt-rock, dirge, ballad. Big G's Deli, an iconic Maine eatery, offered a roast beef, pastrami, and onion ring sandwich called the Hermit, advertised as containing "all locally stolen ingredients." A Dutch artist created a series of oil paintings based on Knight's story and showed them in a gallery in Germany.

Hundreds of journalists, across the United States and the world, attempted to contact him. *The New York Times* compared him to Boo Radley, the recluse in *To Kill a Mockingbird*. TV talk shows solicited his presence. A documentary film team arrived in town.

Every coffee shop and barroom in central Maine, it seemed, was host to a hermit debate. In many cultures hermits have long been considered founts of wisdom, explorers of life's great mysteries. In others they're seen as cursed by the devil. What did Knight wish to tell us? What secrets had he uncovered? Or was he just crazy? What punishment, if any, should he receive? How had he survived? Was his story even true? And if so, why would a man remove himself so profoundly from society? The Kennebec County district attorney, Maeghan Maloney, said that Knight, who apparently wished to spend his entire life anonymous, had become "the most famous person in the state of Maine."

Knight himself, the hub of the commotion, resumed his silence. He did not issue a single word publicly. He accepted no offers—no bail, no wife, no poem, no cash. The five hundred or so dollars sent to him were placed in a restitution fund for victims of his thefts. Before his arrest the hermit had seemed completely inexplicable, but to most people his capture only enhanced the puzzle. The truth felt stranger than the myth.

7

I learned about Christopher Knight while scanning the news on my phone one morning, amid the din and spilled orange juice of my children. The story grabbed me. I've slept hundreds of nights in the wild, most of them before my wife and I had three babies in three years, an experience that bestows various blessings, though not one permitting much quiet time in the forest. I wasn't jealous of Knight's feat—the no-campfire rule is too brutal—but I did feel some degree of respect and a great deal of astonishment.

I like being alone. My preferred exercise is solo long-distance running, and my job, as a journalist and writer, is often asocial. When life becomes overwhelming, my first thought—my fantasy—is to head for the woods. My house is a testament to runaway consumerism, but what I crave most is simplicity and freedom. Once, when my kids were all in diapers and the chaos and sleeplessness had turned poisonous, I did quit the world, albeit briefly and formally, and with the grudging consent of my wife. I fled to India and enrolled in a ten-day silent retreat, hoping that a large dose of alone time would settle my nerves.

It didn't. The retreat was secular, though heavy on meditation—we were taught an ancient style of self-contemplation known as Vipassana—and I found it grueling. It was more monastic than eremitic, with hundreds of other attendees, but we were not allowed to talk or gesture or make eye contact. The desire to socialize never left me, and simply sitting still was a physical struggle. Still, the ten days were enough for me to see, as if peering over the edge of a well, that silence could be mystical, and that if you dared, diving fully into your inner depths might be both profound and disturbing.

I didn't dare—scrutinizing oneself that candidly seemed to require bravery and fortitude I didn't possess, as well as a tremendous amount of free time. But I never stopped thinking about what might reside down there, what insights, what truth. There were people at the retreat in India who had completed months of silent withdrawal, and the calmness and placidity they radiated made me envious. Knight had seemingly surpassed all boundaries, plunging to the bottom of the well, to the mysterious deep.

Then there was the matter of books. Knight clearly loved to read. He stole, according to news reports, a lot of science fiction and spy novels and best sellers and even Harlequin romances—whatever was available in the cabins of North Pond—but one person also lost a finance textbook, a scholarly World War II tome, and James Joyce's *Ulysses*. During his arrest, Knight mentioned his admiration for Daniel Defoe's *Robinson Crusoe*. Crusoe lived on his island almost exactly as long as Knight lived in the woods, though he had his man Friday for several years. Also, the story's fictitious. Maeghan

Maloney, the local DA, said that Knight was now reading *Gulliver's Travels* in jail.

Two of life's greatest pleasures, by my reckoning, are camping and reading—most gloriously, both at once. The hermit appeared to have the same passions on an exponentially grander scale. I thought about Knight as I vacuumed the breakfast crumbs, and I thought about him as I paid bills in my office. I worried that someone with no immunity to our lifestyle, physically or mentally, was now being exposed to all our germs. And more than anything, I was eager to hear what he'd reveal.

Nothing, it turned out. The reporters moved on to other matters, and the documentary team packed up and went home. My mind still swirled, my curiosity kindled. Two months after his arrest, in the late-evening calm of a house filled with sleepers, I sat at my desk and harnessed my thoughts. I took out a yellow pad of lined paper and a smooth-rolling pen.

"Dear Mr. Knight," I began. "I'm writing to you from western Montana, where I have lived for nearly twenty-five years. I've read a few newspaper stories about you, and I felt strongly compelled to write you a letter."

Everything I'd learned about him, I continued, had only triggered more questions. I added that I was an avid outdoorsman and that we were both in the same middle-aged part of life—I was forty-four years old, three years younger than him. I informed Knight that I was a journalist, and I photocopied a few of my recent magazine articles, including a piece on a hunter-gatherer tribe in remote East Africa whose isolation I thought might appeal to him. I mentioned my love of books and divulged that Ernest Hemingway was one of my favorites.

"I hope you are coping okay in your new situation," I wrote in the final paragraph of the two-and-a-half-page letter. "And I hope, too, that your legal situation is resolved in as gentle a manner as possible." I signed off, "Yours, Mike."

8

A white envelope arrived in my mailbox a week later, the address printed in blue ink with wobbly block letters. The return address read "Chris Knight." A rubber-stamped message on the back delivered a warning: "This correspondence is forwarded from the Kennebec County Jail. Contents have not been evaluated."

Inside the envelope was a single sheet of paper, folded in thirds. Smoothing it flat on my desk, I saw it was from the article I'd mailed him about the tribe known as the Hadza, who live in the Rift Valley of Tanzania. The story had appeared in *National Geographic,* and I'd included color copies of the photographs along with my text.

Knight had returned one of the images, a portrait of a Hadza elder named Onwas. The article mentioned that Onwas was about sixty years old and had lived his entire life in the bush, camping with an extended family of two dozen. Onwas did not keep track of years, only seasons and moons. He lived with just a handful of possessions, enjoyed abundant leisure time, and represented one of the final links to the deepest root of the human family tree.

Our genus, *Homo,* arose two and a half million years ago, and for more than ninety-nine percent of human existence, we all lived like Onwas, in small bands of nomadic hunter-gatherers. Though the groups may have been tight-knit and communal, nearly everyone, anthropologists conjecture, spent significant parts of their lives surrounded by quiet, either alone or with a few others, foraging for edible plants and stalking prey in the wild. This is who we truly are.

The agricultural revolution began twelve thousand years ago, in the Fertile Crescent of the Middle East, and the planet was swiftly reorganized into villages and cities and nations, and soon the average person spent virtually no time alone at all. To a thin but steady stream of people, this was unacceptable, so they escaped. Recorded history extends back five thousand years, and for as long as humans have been writing, we have been writing about hermits. It's a primal fascination. Chinese texts etched on animal bones, as well as the clay tablets containing the *Epic of Gilgamesh,* a poem from Mesopotamia dating to around 2000 B.C., refer to shamans or wild men residing alone in the woods.

People have sought out solitary existences at all times across all cultures, some revered and some despised. Confucius, who died in 479 B.C., seems to have spoken in praise of hermits— some, he said, as recorded by his disciples, had achieved great virtue. In the third and fourth centuries A.D., thousands of hermits, devout Christians known as the Desert Fathers and Desert Mothers, moved into the limestone caves on both banks of the Nile River in Egypt. The nineteenth century brought Thoreau; the twentieth, the Unabomber.

None of these hermits remained secluded as long as Knight

did, at least not without significant help from assistants, or without being corralled into a monastery or convent, which is what happened to the Desert Fathers and Mothers. There might have existed—or, it's possible, currently exist—hermits more completely hidden than Knight, but if so, they have never been found. Capturing Knight was the human equivalent of netting a giant squid. His seclusion was not pure, he was a thief, but he persisted for twenty-seven years while speaking a total of one word and never touching anyone else. Christopher Knight, you could argue, is the most solitary known person in all of human history.

Mailing me the photo of Onwas seemed Knight's way of sending a shrewdly opaque message, hinting at admiration for someone else who'd spent his life away from modern society, expressed without using a single word. Then I turned the page over and saw that Knight had written on the back. The note was brief—three paragraphs, two hundred and seventy-three words, the lines crowded together as if for warmth. Still, it contained some of the first statements Knight had shared with anyone in the world.

"Received your letter, obviously," he opened, without salutation. His use of the word "obviously"—droll, patronizing—elicited a smile. He was replying to my letter, he explained, in the hope that writing back would provide some relief from the "stress and boredom" of his incarceration. Also, he didn't feel comfortable speaking: "My vocal, verbal skills have become rather rusty and slow." He apologized for his sloppy penmanship; a regular pen can be used as a weapon, so he was permitted only one with a bendable rubber casing in jail.

Knight was shy about everything, it seemed, except literary criticism. He wrote that he felt "rather lukewarm" about Ernest Hemingway. He was partial to history and biography, he said, though he was presently interested in Rudyard Kipling, preferably his "lesser known works." Here he added, as if clarifying why he stole so many potboilers, that he would read just about anything when the alternative was nothing.

He was aware of the commotion his arrest had stirred— all the letters that were mailed to him were duly delivered to his cell, though the majority of them were, he noted, "crazy, creepy, just plain strange." He had selected mine to answer, he implied, because it wasn't particularly creepy, and because he'd sensed something pleasing in the words I'd chosen to use. As if catching himself getting a little friendly, he abruptly wrote that he didn't wish to reveal anything more.

He then seemed concerned that he was now being too unfriendly. "I wince at the rudeness of this reply but think it better to be clear and honest rather than polite. Tempted to say 'nothing personal,' but handwritten letters are always personal, whatever their content." He ended with: "It was kind of you to write. Thank you." He did not sign his name.

I wrote back promptly, and mail-ordered for him a couple of Kiplings (*The Man Who Would Be King* and *Captains Courageous*). Knight had said in his letter that because he didn't know me, he would write only "innocuous content." This seemed an invitation to become less of a stranger, so I filled five pages with personal anecdotes about my family, along with an account of one of my now-infrequent wilderness escapes: the summer solstice had recently occurred around the same time as the so-called supermoon, the year's full moon that is closest to Earth, and I had observed this celestial coupling while camping with a friend amid the mountains of Montana.

Also, I disclosed to Knight that I was a flawed journalist. In 2001, while writing a magazine article about child labor, I wove various interviews together to create a composite character, a storytelling method that is against the rules of journalism. I was caught for my deception, and soon banned from writing for some publications, and for a while I felt isolated and shunned in professional circles. Maybe the admission that I was a sinner within my profession, while Knight was a confessed thief, unable to live in solitude without pilfering from others, would engender a sense of connection—both of us striving, and failing, to achieve lofty ideals.

I was heartened to find his next letter in the mail. It wasn't my misdeed but the camping trip that had struck a chord. He began his three-page note with a description of one of his attempts to practice speaking. He had approached a half dozen of his fellow inmates, many of whom were young and hardened, and tried to initiate a conversation. The topic he had chosen to discuss with them was the pleasing synchronicity of the summer solstice and the supermoon. "I thought it of at least trivial interest," he wrote. "Apparently not. You should have seen the blank looks I got."

Many of the people he attempted to talk with simply nodded and smiled and thought him "stupid or crazy." Or they just stared at him unabashedly, as if he were some oddity on display. Then my letter arrived and he saw that, by serendipity, I'd mentioned the very same topic. He described himself as "startled," and from this point forward his writing was no longer innocuous but instead as candid and poignant as a diary entry.

He felt tormented by jail, locked in his cage with another inmate. "You asked how I sleep. Little and uneasy. I am nearly always tired and nervous." But, he added, in his staccato, almost songlike style, he deserved to be imprisoned. "I stole. I was a thief. I repeatedly stole over many years. I knew it was wrong. Knew it was wrong, felt guilty about it every time, yet continued to do it."

In his next letter, and the one after, he said he found "relief and release" by imagining the woods just beyond the cinder-block walls. He mentioned, in lyrical writing, the growing wildflowers: black-eyed Susans, lady's slippers, clover, even dandelions (though he found these "more interesting dead"). He could almost hear the "song of salt and fat frying" as he cooked on his camp stove. Mostly, he just wished for quiet— "all the quiet I can take, consume, eat, dine upon, savor, relish, feast." Rather than becoming gradually more accustomed to jail, to being around other people, Knight was deteriorating. In the woods, he said, he'd always carefully maintained his facial hair, but now he stopped shaving. "Use my beard," he wrote, "as a jail calendar."

Several more times, he attempted to converse with other inmates. He could "fumble forth" with a few hesitant words, but every subject—music, movies, television—was lost on him, as was all modern slang. He only occasionally used a con-traction, and never a swearword. "You talk like a book," one inmate teased him. The guards and jail authorities, Knight noted, approached him with "pity and a small smile," and everyone seemed to ask him the same question: Do you know who the president is? He did know; he'd regularly listened to the news on a radio while he lived in the woods. "This is their test for me," he wrote. "Always tempted to give a really absurd response. Don't, but tempted."

Soon he essentially stopped talking. "I am retreating into silence as a defensive mode," he mentioned. Eventually, he was down to uttering just five words, and only to guards: yes; no; please; thank you. "I am surprised," he wrote, "by the amount of respect this garners me. That silence intimidates puzzles me. Silence is to me normal, comfortable." Later he added, "I will admit to feeling a little contempt for those who can't keep quiet."

He shared only brief details about his time in the woods, but what he did reveal was harrowing. Some years, he made it clear, he barely survived the winter. In one letter, he said that to get through difficult times, he tried meditating. "I didn't meditate every day, month, season in the woods. Just when death was near. Death in the form of too little food or too much cold for too long." Meditation worked, he concluded: "I am alive and sane, at least I think I'm sane." Again there was no formal closing. His letters simply ended, sometimes in mid-thought.

He returned to the theme of sanity in a following letter: "When I came out of the woods they applied the hermit label to me. Strange idea to me. I had never thought of myself as a hermit. Then I got worried. For I knew with the label hermit comes the idea of crazy. See the ugly little joke."

Even worse, he feared that his time in jail would only prove correct those who thought him insane. His legal proceedings were mired in delays, and after four months in jail Knight had no clue what punishment awaited. A sentence of a dozen or more years was possible. "Stress levels sky high," he wrote. "Give me a number. How long? Months? Years? How long in prison for me? Tell me the worst. How long?"

The uncertainty wore on him. The conditions in jail—the handcuffs, the noise, the filth, the crowding—mangled his senses. It's likely that, if one must be incarcerated in the United States, a jail in central Maine would be among the more tolerable spots, but to Knight it was torture. "Bedlam" is how he referred to the place. It never got dark in jail; at eleven p.m., the lights merely became a little duller. "I suspect," he noted, "more damage has been done to my sanity in jail, in months; than years, decades, in the woods."

Finally, he decided that he could not even write. "For a while writing relieved stress for me. No longer." He sent one last, crushing letter, the fifth he'd mailed me over the course of eight weeks; in it, he seemed at the verge of breakdown. "Still tired. More tired. Tireder, tiredest, tired ad nauseum, tired infinitium."

And that was it. He ceased writing. I mailed him three letters over the next three weeks—"How are you holding up?" I worried—but no wobbly-addressed white envelopes appeared in my mailbox. I reread his final letter, hoping to unearth some subliminal message. I did not. But the closing lines clutched at me. For the only time in our summer-long correspondence, he had signed his name. Despite the exhaustion and the tension, the last words he'd penned were wry and self-mocking: "Your friendly neighborhood Hermit, Christopher Knight."

9

Augusta, Maine, is picturesque but a little melancholy, the downtown streets empty, the factories along the Kennebec River that once produced broom handles and headstones and shoes now giant brick skeletons. The jail was built in 1858. The original structure, a small granite fortress, has become the sheriff's department offices, and Knight was incarcerated in the attached addition, a three-story slab of pale gray cinder blocks.

Visiting hours begin most evenings at six forty-five. I arrived early and passed through two sets of metal doors on the ground floor, into the jail's waiting room. I stood at a narrow desk before a mirrored window made of one-way glass, wondering if I needed to press a button to get a person's attention. A sign beside a giant pump dispenser of hand sanitizer instructed visitors to use some before entering the facility.

"Who you here to see?" squawked an amplified voice from the other side of the glass.

"Christopher Knight."

"Relationship?"

"Friend," I answered, unconfidently. He didn't know I was here, and I had doubts that he would agree to a visit. His letters had hinted at great suffering and greater fortitude, as well as a singular story untold, and once it had become clear that he was no longer writing, I'd taken a chance and flown east, Montana to Maine.

A metal drawer popped open, and identification was demanded. I deposited my driver's license, and the drawer snapped shut. When the license was returned, I sat on a bench in the waiting room, buzzing and slamming sounds reverberating through the dirty white walls.

An elderly couple checked in, followed by a man who answered "I'm his father" to the relationship question, then sat down clutching a bag of underwear as if it were a lifeline. Underwear, in its original packaging, is one of the few items you can give to an inmate at the Kennebec County jail. Then came a woman with two young girls in matching pink dresses. The girls looked as though they had chicken pox, but the mother explained, to no one in particular, that it was just mosquito bites. "We live way out in the woods," she added. This reminded me to ask Knight, if I did see him, how he had coped with insects, which can be savage in the northern forests. Even Henry David Thoreau, not known for kvetching, wrote in *The Maine Woods* that he was "seriously molested" by bugs.

Eventually a baby-faced corrections officer appeared, carrying a handheld metal detector. He called out a name, and the elderly couple stood. The officer worked the detector, unlocked a maroon door labeled VISITING 1, and shut it behind them. Then he sent the man with the underwear into VISITING 2.

There were three visiting rooms, and when a third name was announced and the woman and children rose, I was dismayed. But then the officer reopened VISITING 2, ushered the group in, and called, "Knight."

I was wanded front and back, thankful that the small notebook and pen stashed in my pocket weren't confiscated. The officer unlocked VISITING 3—a sign on the door warned that if you left for any reason, you'd be prohibited from returning—and I stepped inside and the door closed behind me, and I was rattled with nerves. My eyes adjusted to the dimmer light, and there, in the tiny booth, sealed off behind a thick pane of shatterproof plastic, sitting on a stool, was Christopher Knight.

Rarely in my life have I witnessed someone less pleased to see me. His thin lips were pulled into a downturned scowl; his eyes did not rise to meet mine. I sat across from him, also on a stool with a black wooden top. I placed my notebook on the metal desk bolted to the wall below the plastic window. There was no acknowledgment of my presence, not the merest nod. He gazed someplace beyond my left shoulder, nearly motionless. He was wearing a dull green overlaundered jail uniform several sizes too big.

A black phone receiver hung on the wall, and I picked it up. He picked his up—the first movement I saw him make. There was a bit of recorded legal boilerplate, warning that the conversation might be monitored, and then the lines opened.

I spoke first. "Nice to meet you, Chris."

He didn't respond. He just sat there, stone-faced, his balding head shining like a snowfield beneath the fluorescent lights, his beard—his jail calendar, one hundred and forty days in—a mess of curls, most brown, some red, a few gray. He had on metal-framed bifocals, different from the glasses he'd worn forever in the woods. His broad forehead and pointy beard gave his face a triangular appearance, like a yield sign. He looked a little bit like the Russian writer Leo Tolstoy. He was skinny.

The only picture I'd seen of Knight before coming was his mug shot, in which he was clean-shaven and slightly frowning, wearing his old clunky glasses, his eyes behind them heavy-lidded and dull after the exhaustion and stress of his arrest. The man in front of me now appeared no more welcoming, but there was a clear sense of alertness and energy. He might not be looking at me, but he was surely observing, though I didn't know if he'd speak even a single word.

Knight had mentioned repeatedly in his letters that he felt at ease in silence. I looked at him not looking at me. He had pale, boiled-potato-colored skin and a sharp nose. His shoulders drooped, his posture curled inward, defensive. Maybe a minute passed.

This was all I could endure. "The constant banging and buzzing in here," I said, "must be so jarring compared with the sounds of nature." He shifted his eyes to me—a minor victory—then glanced away. His eyes were light brown, and rather small. He scarcely had any eyebrows. My comment hung in the air.

Then he spoke, or at least his mouth moved. His first words were inaudible. He was holding the phone's mouthpiece too low, below his chin. It had been decades since he'd regularly used a phone; he was out of practice. I indicated with my hand that he needed to move it up. He did, then repeated his pronouncement.

"It's jail," he said, and nothing else. Silence once more.

There were so many questions to ask him, but they all seemed wrong—too prying, too personal. I tried an innocuous one: "What season did you like best when you were living in the woods?"

Knight paused, apparently laboring to create a response. "I take each season as it comes," he said, his scowl reappearing. His voice was raspy, each word a distinct entity—overenunciated, unnaturally spaced, absent of elisions. Just a procession of nearly toneless sounds, with a hint of the stretched vowels of a Down East accent.

I plowed awkwardly on. "Have you made any friends in jail?"

"No," he said.

I shouldn't have come. He didn't want me there; I didn't feel comfortable being there. But the jail had granted me a one-hour visit, and I resolved to stay. I settled atop my stool, feeling hyperaware of all my gestures, my facial expressions, my breathing. No one could out-silence Knight, but I at least wanted to make an effort. The lights in the room were flickery, and a couple of ceiling tiles were missing. Knight's right leg, I saw through the scratched window, was bouncing rapidly. The floor on the visitor's side of the booth was covered in pale red industrial carpeting; his side, blue.

He had written in one of his letters that meeting people often made his "skin crawl," and indeed he was scratching his forearms. He had a nebulous brown birthmark on the back of his freckled right hand; a few stray wisps of hair coiled up from his crown like snakes being charmed. Someone had graffitied "let me out" in black ink on one of the walls, and another person had scratched "187" onto the door, which is a slang term for murder, based on the California penal code.

My patience was rewarded. First, after a couple of minutes, his leg settled down. He quit scratching. And then, as if he'd finally found equilibrium with his surroundings, Knight began to come to life.

"Some people want me to be this warm and fuzzy person," he said. "All filled with friendly hermit wisdom. Just spouting off fortune-cookie lines from my hermit home."

Everything he said was clear, though extremely soft. I had to plug my non-phone ear with my finger to hear him. His gestures were minimal. But his words, when he deigned to share them, could be imaginative and entertaining. And caustic.

"Your hermit home—like under a bridge?" I said, trying to play along.

He embarked on an achingly long blink. "You're thinking of a troll."

I laughed, and his face moved in the direction of a smile. We had made a connection, or at least the awkwardness of our introduction had softened. We began to converse somewhat normally, though never at a rapid clip. Knight seemed to weigh the precision of every word he used, careful as a poet. Even his handwritten letters had gone through at least one rough draft, he said, mostly to remove unnecessary insults. Only necessary ones remained.

He explained about the lack of eye contact. "I'm not used

to seeing people's faces. There's too much information there. Aren't you aware of it? Too much, too fast." Following his cue, I looked over his shoulder while he stared over mine. We maintained this arrangement for much of the visit. "I don't like people touching me," he added. He was able to endure the occasional pat-downs by guards, and that was all. "You're not a hugger," he asked, "are you?"

I admitted that I do at times participate in embraces.

"I'm glad this is between us," he said, tapping on the window. "If there was a set of blinds here, I'd close them." The jail authorities had given him the option of a contact visit, but he'd chosen this style instead. "I prefer a meeting of the minds rather than a touching of bodies. I like my distance."

Knight seemed to say exactly what he was thinking, raw and true, unfiltered by the safety net of social niceties. There was no little-white-lie mechanism in him—the one that deems the meal at a dinner party delicious no matter the taste, the one that keeps the gears of human interaction well oiled. "I'm not sorry about being rude if it gets to the point quicker," he said.

Here's what he had written in a letter about an author photo of mine he'd seen in the sample packet of writing I'd mailed him: "You look particularly nerdy. Next time have your wife pick the picture." When I mentioned during the visit that my son's name is Beckett, he said, "Ugh. Terrible. Why did you name him that? He's going to hate you when he gets older."

He said that when he was told I'd come to the jail, his first instinct was to turn down the visit. But we'd already formed an epistolary relationship, and my presence might allow him to practice holding a conversation, a skill that had so far eluded him in jail. Also I'd simply shown up—I don't think any other journalist had, including the documentary crew— and he knew I lived far away. It would have been rude of him, he felt, to refuse my visit, so he'd accepted it, and then was rude to my face.

Knight could seem prickly—he *is* prickly—but he also said that since his capture, he'd found himself emotionally over- whelmed at unexpected moments. "Like TV commercials have made me teary. It's not a good thing in jail to have people see you crying."

He wondered how he was being portrayed in the media. "Is it like at the end of the radio newscast, when they have the weird stories? World's largest pumpkin grown, and man emerges from Maine woods after twenty-seven years." He asked if everyone really was calling him a hermit, and I told him they were. All the local papers, the *Kennebec Journal,* the *Morning Sentinel,* the *Portland Press Herald,* sometimes referred to him as the hermit. "I don't like the term, but I understand," said Knight. "There is a certain accuracy to it. 'Hermit' does fit the bill. It's not like I could stop it, anyway."

He saw a strategic opening here. The media was apparently clamoring to view a real live hermit, and Knight, by growing out his beard wildly, had provided the character they envi- sioned. His facial hair served not just as a calendar but also as a mask, absorbing the stares of others while allowing him a little privacy in plain sight. "I can hide behind it, I can play to stereotypes and assumptions. One of the benefits of being labeled a hermit is that it permits me strange behavior."

He needed to prepare for "re-entry into society," as he put it, and was worried that he'd be seen only as a madman. He was seeking help—he understood that his behavior was strange and hoped to change it—so I asked that he look at me. His eyes darted all over; there were no welcoming facial motions, no gestures, no interaction. Not so much as a raised eyebrow. A newborn baby can dance this way but Knight couldn't sustain it for more than a few moments.

I finally caught his eyes and asked him the waiting-room question—"What did you do when the mosquitoes were bad?"—and he said, "I used bug spray," and turned away. My presence was a burden to him. It seemed that all Knight desired was to be left alone. Even so, just before time expired on our visit, I asked if I could visit again.

His answer was unexpected. He said, "Yes."

10

Knight lived in the same campsite for nearly his entire time in the woods. The site is in a surprising spot. Maine itself, the cork atop a fizz of small states crowding the American Northeast, contains vast realms of uninhabited woodlands, mostly owned by timber companies, but Knight chose to disappear well within the bounds of society. Towns and roads and houses surround his site; he could overhear canoeists' conversations on North Pond. He wasn't so much removed from humanity as sitting on the sidelines. From the nearest cabin to his hiding spot is a three-minute walk, if you know where you're going.

Only Knight had known where he was going. But on the evening he was captured, before heading to jail, he shared his secret. He guided the arresting officers, Sergeant Hughes and Trooper Vance, to his hiding place. The site is on private property, and the landowner didn't want the place to become a tourist attraction, though word of the location leaked out.

A local handyman, Carroll Bubar, who'd followed the police footprints through the snow to Knight's camp, gave me cryptic instructions, and I drove north out of Augusta into the heartland of Maine, the road tucked like a river between tree-covered ridges. It's cow-and-horse country, stretches of rolling farmland separating one-stoplight towns. A couple of general stores are named General Store; live bait worms are for sale in plastic containers, refrigerated next to the milk. French names are stenciled on mailboxes, Poulin and Thibodeau and Leclair—descendants, most likely, of the Acadians, the French colonists who settled in the New World in the seventeenth and eighteenth centuries. In the region's original charter, from 1664, King Charles II of England granted rule to his brother James, the Duke of York, over an area referred to as "the maine land of New England," a phrase that probably determined the name of the state after it separated from Massachusetts in 1820.

A narrow washboarded road passes the driveway to the Pine Tree Camp, then leads to a locked gate. From here, a few minutes of walking offered the first glimpse of the water, ripples flashing silver in the sun. There are two ponds in the neighborhood, Little North tucked like a child against North, connected by a narrow passage—a total of nearly four square miles of water, clean and cold. Most of the cabins are set back in the trees and are hard to see.

It was midweek, toward summer's end, and the area was quiet. With a couple of exceptions, the vacation homes along the shoreline—"camps," they're called, self-effacingly—are simple affairs, unfancy inside and out, several in need of new siding. In many living rooms, mounted deer heads are the principal decor. There are large outdoor fire pits, floating docks, a scattering of kayaks and canoes. A wind chime made of empty beer cans hangs on a tree. Across a small stream is a weatherworn camp with a metal roof, sided with hemlock board and batten that was hewn from trees on the lot. This is the place three minutes from the campsite.

Here, a muddy driveway forms one of the borders of Knight's forest. Though, of course, it's not his forest. Every night of his stay he was illegally trespassing. I was likewise trespassing, and had resolved to keep as quiet as possible. Knight's campsite was somewhere on a two-hundred-and-twenty-acre parcel, with one year-round house on it, from which Knight never stole. It's a large piece of property, but the North Pond area sees a regular procession of hikers and hunters and cross-country skiers, and the community hosts an annual boat parade, ice-fishing derby, and loon count. With all these people around, it seemed strange that Knight's spot remained unknown for so long. Perhaps there was a good explanation.

As I stepped off the driveway and into the woods, the mash of trees and shrubs was so dense that the forest held its own humidity. My eyeglasses promptly fogged. The Chris Knight woods are an old-growth multispecies forest, a couple of enormous eastern hemlocks towering above the crowd, the undergrowth bursting with ferns and brilliant red-topped mushrooms. The explanation for the site's secrecy was the jumble of boulders—vehicle-sized, possibly glacier-borne gifts from the last ice age, scattered wildly and everywhere, carpeted with moss and lichen. Half the steps I took required handholds, rocks grabbed for support while branches cracked and crunched, quiet as a car alarm.

Other than central Maine, there are not too many places in the United States that could host a hermit like Knight. The Maine woods are ideally thick—in the western U.S., as well as all of Alaska, the forests are generally far more open—and the population in this part of the state is perfectly distributed, neither too dense nor too widely scattered, either of which could hinder a thieving habit. Plus in Maine there's both a keep-to-yourself ethos and a lax adhesion to private property boundaries, so that if you do happen to spot a stranger walking about, it's common to simply disregard him or her. One North Pond cabin owner who lives most of the year in Texas, where trespassing is less tolerated, said that no one like Knight would have survived undisturbed in the Lone Star State.

The cryptic instructions from the handyman were this: "Keep the late-afternoon sun in your face and walk up the hill." Okay, but there were a dozen little hills back there, and with the boulders it was impossible to move in anything close to a straight line. No paths exist, but summer is rife with mosquitoes and poison ivy and thorns. Pine needles stick to your sweat, and you have to roll down your shirtsleeves to fend off the bugs. You can't see more than a few feet in any direction; it's claustrophobic and disorienting. "The billy-goat woods," Sergeant Hughes called it. The locals' term for this patch of forest, known for repelling hunters and holding snow, is "the Jarsey," sharing a name with the unpaved Jarsey Road, which cuts through it.

I had never lost my bearings in a forest more quickly, so I gave up, fumbled back to the muddy driveway, and sat on a rock to reset, gulping water. The second battle with the Jarsey was no better. Even after carefully aligning myself with the sun—it was, indeed, late afternoon—once again I was soon wandering randomly in the Brillo forest. The third attempt was worse. The moss covering the boulders was damp, slick as ice, and my foot slipped and the weight of my backpack, stuffed with camping gear and food, yanked me off balance. I tumbled face-first, bumping my forehead on a rock with enough force to raise an immediate lump. One of my hiking boots was torn, no match for these woods. Knight walked here all the time. Silently. Without injury. *At night.* How was this possible?

The day before, at his office in the Skowhegan barracks, Sergeant Hughes had sat with perfect posture in his starched green game warden uniform and black combat boots and described what it was like to follow Knight, matching him step for step. Hughes spends much of his workday and a majority of his free time in the woods of Maine. He traps muskrats and foxes, and makes a few dollars on the side selling the pelts. During a missing-person search, he is able to read the woods with a skill verging on clairvoyance. Nobody passes through the trees around North Pond without him knowing it; everyone leaves a trace. With one exception.

When Hughes spoke about his walk with Knight, his gaze lost its intensity. Hughes is a law-and-order man not given to using hyperbole. He was trailing a criminal who had just admitted to a thousand felonies. But he was in awe.

"I never in my life had an experience like that," said Hughes. What he witnessed was a work of art. "Every step was calculated, every movement. He clearly took the same steps all the time, year after year, decade after decade." Hughes said that while Knight was walking, he entered this fugue-like state. "He was in a zone," Hughes said. "He was kind of tuned right out." The trance was so strong that Knight didn't respond when Hughes tried to ask him questions. "I just let him be in the zone," Hughes recalled. "This guy would never step anywhere that would leave a track. He wouldn't break a twig, flatten a fern, kick a mushroom. He avoided all snow. I was beside myself—I couldn't even fathom it. I was in shock. I probably could have blindfolded him and he wouldn't have missed a beat. He moves like a cat."

The more stubbornly Knight's site remained hidden, the greater grew my desire to see it. The sun dropped lower, and a couple of beams lasered through the trees. I moved slowly amid the Jarsey. At each boulder field I performed a little grid search, back and forth, probing with needle-in-a-haystack precision.

I started to form a mental map, noting unusually shaped rocks and distinct clusters of trees. At last, I began to really see the forest. In an area of exceptionally large boulders, the kind geologists might call erratics, there was an elephant-sized stone that, looked at from a certain angle, turned out to be two slightly separated rocks. The appearance of these two rocks as a single boulder was an optical illusion, a trick of the forest. The gap between the rocks was just wide enough so that I could twist my body and slip through, a secret doorway, and I emerged at a dreamlike clearing and there it was.

11

My goodness. Knight had created from the chaos a living-room-sized clearing completely invisible a few steps away, protected by a natural Stonehenge of boulders and a thicket of hemlocks. Tree branches linked overhead to form a trellis, masking his site from the air. This was why Knight's skin was so pale—he'd resided in perpetual shade. "I'm from the woods, not the fields," he'd said about his pallor. The room was large, about twenty feet on each side, with ideally flat ground cleared of stones and situated on a slight rise that allowed just enough breeze to keep the mosquitoes away but not so much as to cause severe windchill in winter. It felt to me as if a cube of forest had disappeared.

"If he wouldn't have shown us his site, we probably never would have found it," said Hughes. "He just darted between these big rocks, and I'm thinking, What the heck is he doing? Then, boom, there's the opening." There were other ways in and out of the site, but they were effectively blocked by dense tangles of downed trees and piles of boulders. The elephant rocks provided the only sensible entrance, and certainly the most dramatic. "We came around the rocks," said Vance, "and my mouth hit the ground and I'm going, Oh my God, it's real."

The police had removed much of Knight's stuff, enough to fill two pickups, and ripped down his tarps and dismantled his tent, which sat crumpled in a sad ball, a couple of poles sticking out like knitting needles. First, though, everything had been photographed in its original state.

"He set his tent east-west," said Hughes, bobbing his head in reluctant approval. "That wasn't an accident. That's based on survivalist training. His site is not on top of a hill, not in a valley. It's halfway between. He's following the principles of Sun Tzu, in *The Art of War.* But this guy was strictly out of high school in a small town, with no military experience at all."

Knight always kept the place fastidiously clean, raking the leaves and shoveling the snow, though it was now, nearly five months after his arrest, covered with pine needles and downed leaves. By clearing off a small area, then scraping away some soil—Hughes had suggested this—I could see, faceup, faded and badly waterlogged, the familiar yellow-bordered cover of a *National Geographic* magazine. The cover line was still legible ("Zaire River") as was the date: November 1991.

The pages flaked away, but there was another issue underneath ("Florida Watershed," July 1990). Then another, and another. A foot down, there were still more. The magazines had been bound with electrical tape into thick bundles that Knight referred to as "bricks." Elsewhere, there were buried bricks of *People,* of *Vanity Fair,* of *Glamour,* of *Playboy.* Knight had recycled his old reading material as subflooring, creating a platform that was perfectly level and also permitted decent drainage of rainwater.

He'd spread a carpet over the magazines, which served as the floor of his interior living area. The walls of his home, the police photos showed, were constructed of brown and green plastic tarps and several large black garbage bags. These were all intricately overlaid, like roof tiles, anchored in place with guylines tied to tree branches and car batteries, forming an A-frame structure a good ten feet tall and twelve feet long, wide open at both ends like a train tunnel. It was an aesthetically pleasing creation, almost churchlike in appearance, that blended into the color palette of the forest. It'd be hard to make something nicer solely of tarps and garbage bags.

The entrance to his structure closest to the elephant rocks brought you into Knight's kitchen: a Coleman two-burner camp stove atop a couple of milk crates, with a green five-gallon bucket as a seat. A garden hose, repurposed as a gas line, was attached to the stove and snaked out the shelter to a propane tank. The stove ventilated through the shelter's open ends. Cooking supplies were hung from ropes along the kitchen walls—a frying pan, a mug, a roll of paper towels, a spatula, a strainer, a pot. Each item had its own hook. A couple of mousetraps guarded the floor; a bottle of Purell stood beside a portable cooler. His pantry was a rodent-proof plastic storage container.

Behind the kitchen, toward the other end of the shelter, was Knight's bedroom—a dome-shaped nylon camping tent set up within the A-frame, for added protection from rain and camouflage for the brightly colored tent. Inside the nylon tent, more plastic bins served as closet space. Knight said that he had been embarrassed to show Hughes and Vance his site, not because it was filled with stolen merchandise but because it wasn't clean enough. His tent walls had started to rot and disintegrate, something that happened over time. "It was like someone coming over to your mother's house before she'd had a chance to clean," said Knight. He had already taken a new tent, but he hadn't yet set it up. Like any home owner, Knight was forever toying with ideas for improvements and renovations. He had planned, before he'd been arrested, to add a layer of gravel between the carpet and the magazine bricks, to further prevent rainwater from pooling beneath the floor of his A-frame.

An artificial-grass doormat sat before the tent's door. Knight lived an unspeakably rugged existence but slept rather royally. His bed was composed of a twin-sized mattress and box spring on a metal bed frame, its legs propped on blocks of wood to prevent them from punching holes in the tent floor. There were fitted sheets and real pillows—at the time of his arrest, he was using Tommy Hilfiger pillowcases—and sleeping bags piled up for warmth.

Milk crates worked as nightstands, heaped with books and magazines. He had dozens of wristwatches, flashlights, and portable radios. He had taken extra boots, sleeping bags, and jackets. "I like backup systems, redundancies, and options," he explained. He'd also set up a weather station, a digital receiver wired to an outside temperature gauge, so he knew how cold it was without getting out of bed. His structure was so well designed that his tent never got wet.

On the perimeter of his site, beside the kitchen entry to the tarp structure, a low, flat-topped rock served as Knight's wash area, for himself and his clothes. Here he stored laundry detergent and soap, shampoo and razors. There was, as he'd insisted, no mirror. He liked to steal Axe brand deodorant. He never had a warm shower in twenty-seven years, but he did dump buckets of cold water over his head.

Near the wash area, he'd lashed a tarp, flat but at a downward angle, to four trees. This acted as a giant funnel for rainwater, which he collected in plastic thirty-gallon garbage cans. He generally stored sixty to ninety gallons, enough to get through most dry spells. During severe drought years, he hiked to the shore to fetch lake water, which was clean enough to drink. When the water in his garbage bins became soiled with caterpillar droppings or downed leaves, what Knight called "tree dandruff," he'd strain it through a coffee filter before drinking it. Eventually, the water would turn greenish and a bit slimy, after which Knight used it for laundry or bathing, or boiled it and made tea.

His bathroom, on the camp's rear edge, farthest from the elephant-rocks entrance, was a couple of logs framing an open pit. Knight kept a bathroom kit in his shelter, usually stocked with toilet paper and hand sanitizer. As he'd insisted, there was no fire ring, not a charred piece of wood.

The largest trees around his site had served as storage units. Knight had wrapped thick ropes around a dozen hemlock trunks and tucked items into them—lengths of wire, bungee cords, rusty bedsprings, plastic bags, scissors, a tube of Super Glue, a pair of work gloves, a bent key. "The key could be used as a hook, or to pry something up, as a makeshift screwdriver,

I don't know. I couldn't bring myself to throw anything away. I'm a saver and repurposer." He'd strung clotheslines between trees; typically drying were Knight's staples: dark sweatpants, flannel shirts, and water-resistant jackets and pants.

He'd slid his boots onto sawed-off branches, a wilderness drying rack. One tree had held rakes and snow shovels; another, an olive-green baseball cap and a floppy gray fishing hat. Some items had been in place so long that the trees grew around them. A claw hammer was nearly swallowed by a tree trunk, impossible to remove, and Hughes said that this hammer, more than anything, made him realize how long Knight had lived there.

There was always the chance, Knight had understood, that someone might hike nearby or search for him by air, so he'd tried either to cover any objects that could glint in the sun or to keep them hidden inside the tarp structure. He'd spray-painted a camouflage pattern on plastic coolers and metal garbage cans and on the outside of his spaghetti pot. He kept the blade of his snow shovel, when he wasn't using it, covered with a dark garbage bag, and he'd wrapped the handle in black duct tape. Propane tanks were also stored in garbage bags. In a couple of spots where one might catch a glimpse of his site after the leaves fell, he'd hung camo-colored tarps. He had even painted his clothespins green.

On a little raised area in his camp, a sort of porch, was a green aluminum lawn chair, the bottom of the legs swaddled in duct tape to stop them from sinking into the soft soil. The chair, like everything in his camp, seemed ideally and harmoniously placed to maximize the site's sense of tranquillity.

Knight scoffed at this notion when we later discussed it: "Do you think I was engaging in feng shui?"

I set up my own tent at the site, then sat in the green aluminum chair as chipmunks raced among the trees, acorns dropping through the branches like pachinko balls. A gust of wind bent the high boughs but scattered only a few leaves around the camp.

Night fell fast. Frogs cleared their throats; cicadas whirred like table saws. A woodpecker hammered for grubs. At last came the call of the loons, the theme song of the North Woods, pealing like a laugh or cry, depending on your mood. A car crunched over a dirt road, a dog barked. For a while people could be heard talking, though their words were too muffled to make out.

Knight lived so close to others that he couldn't even sneeze aloud. There's fine cell-phone reception at his site. Civilization was *right there,* hot showers and creature comforts just steps away.

Soon it grew truly dark—one's eyes could be open or closed with hardly a difference—and something moved through the forest. An animal, probably no bigger than a rabbit, though it sounded like a hippo. A couple of stars were visible through the scrim of branches overhead, and the crooked smile of a quarter moon. A bird peeped percussively. Then there was nothing.

It was the kind of total quiet that literally made my ears ring; there was not so much as a breeze. Knight, I envisioned, was cowering on his bunk amid the slamming doors of jail, and I felt like an intruder—not on private property but at his home. I retreated to my tent, feet cold, and turned off my phone and burrowed into my sleeping bag.

A volley of birdcalls greeted the morning. I unzipped my tent. There was mist in the treetops; spider webs shone cat's cradle in the dew. Leaves dropped lazily. Autumn was coming, and the air smelled like sap. I turned on my phone and realized I'd rested for twelve hours, my longest sleep in years.

12

Before Christopher Knight stayed in the woods for a quarter century straight, he never once spent the night in a tent. He grew up less than an hour's drive east of his campsite, in the village of Albion, two thousand people and four thousand cows. Chris is the fifth child and fifth son of Joyce and Sheldon Knight, following Daniel, Joel, Jonathan, and Timothy; he also has a younger sister, Susanna. His sister, according to Chris, has Down syndrome. Joyce raised the kids, and Sheldon, a navy veteran who served in Korea, worked in a creamery, washing out tanker trucks. They lived in a basic two-story farmhouse with a screened-in front porch, on sixty wooded acres with apple trees and raspberry bushes.

The Knight children had old-school chores. "We were country people," said Chris. They split logs to feed their home's wood-burning stove, and picked berries for Joyce's jellies and jams, and tended the family's two-acre garden, which they tilled with a tractor.

Under their father's tutelage, Chris and his brothers learned to fix what was broken, electrical to automotive, and build what they wanted. One family project was a hut, designed by Sheldon and constructed among a stand of cedars on their property. It's both functional and artistic. The walls are made of stone, every rock gathered by one of the boys and carefully stacked and cemented in place. A stove was fashioned from a fifty-five-gallon oil drum, vented with a homemade pipe; the hut was an ideal shelter during deer hunts.

Evenings at the Knight residence were usually devoted to reading, each parent in a rocking chair, book in hand. A family friend, Kerry Vigue, said that the inside of the house looked like a library. The Knights subscribed to magazines such as *Organic Gardening* and *Mother Earth News,* and they owned the entire *Foxfire* series of books, which detail rural skills like tanning hides and keeping bees. Chris said that as a child he tore through dozens of Time-Life history books, available at his elementary school library.

Joyce and Sheldon expected academic excellence from their sons, and they received it. Former high school teachers and classmates all described the Knight boys as uncommonly bright; "a family of brainiacs," one recalled. More prized by his parents than good grades, Chris mentioned, was "Yankee ingenuity"—putting your smarts to work. "It's better to be tough than strong, better to be clever than intelligent," he said, repeating a family maxim. "I was tough and clever."

The family frequently experimented with new varieties of seeds, to maximize yield. They grew potatoes, beans, pumpkins, and corn. "Basic stuff to fill the bellies of a bunch of boys," said Chris.

The Knights also studied thermodynamics, then built a

small greenhouse, where they buried hundreds of one-gallon milk jugs, filled with water, just below ground level, creating what's known as a heat sink. Due to the nature of the electro-magnetic bonds in water molecules—chemists refer to such molecules as "sticky"—water can store about four times more thermal energy than soil. During the day, the water buried in the Knight family greenhouse absorbed heat; after sunset, it slowly released energy. Using this system, they grew food all winter and didn't need to pay a dime to the power com-pany to heat the greenhouse. "In my family," said Chris, "self-education, self-improvement was preferred."

Money was tight. Whenever Sheldon came home with coins in his pocket, he dropped them in a coffee can, and Joyce dis-tributed them in the morning before school, for milk money. They never got rid of scrap metal or spare parts.

Chris described his family as "obsessed with privacy." He begged that they not be contacted or disturbed, at least while he was still in jail. The Knights socialized with a small group of friends and relatives, and virtually no one else. One's desire to be alone, biologists have found, is partially genetic and to some degree measurable. If you have low levels of the pitu-itary peptide oxytocin—sometimes called the master chemical of sociability—and high quantities of the hormone vasopres-sin, which may suppress your need for affection, you tend to require fewer interpersonal relationships.

"Each of us inherits from our parents a certain level of need for social inclusion," wrote John Cacioppo in his book *Loneli-ness*. Cacioppo, the director of the Center for Cognitive and Social Neuroscience at the University of Chicago, said that everyone naturally possesses a "genetic thermostat for connection." Chris Knight's must be set near absolute zero.

Sheldon, Chris's father, died in 2001—Chris didn't know that until his arrest, more than a dozen years later—but Joyce, in her eighties, still lives in the same house, along with her daughter, for whom she remains the caretaker. The oldest son, Daniel, ten years older than Chris, resides in a double-wide mobile home on an adjoining lot. Their closest neighbor, John Boivin, said he's lived next door to the Knights for fourteen years and still hasn't said hello to anyone in the family. Sometimes Boivin spots Joyce collecting the newspaper. Chris's sister, Susanna, has hardly been seen in public for decades.

"I know everyone in Albion," said Amanda Dow, who has worked in the local town office for close to two decades, "but I can't put a face to them." People who knew Sheldon invariably described him as introverted. Bob Milliken, an Albion dairy farmer and distant cousin of Sheldon's, said the Knight family was "smart, honest, hardworking, self-sufficient, well respected, and quiet." Milliken added that on the rare occasions when he did speak with anyone in the family, he "more or less just stuck to talking about the weather."

Chris insisted that he'd had a fine youth. "No complaints. I had good parents." No one else in his family has had any trouble with the law. Two of Knight's brothers, Joel and Timothy, visited him in jail, the only members of the family to do so. Chris didn't recognize them, he admitted; only Joel's laugh sounded familiar. The brothers said they'd often wondered what had happened to Chris. They had supposed he was dead but had never expressed this thought to their mother.

They'd always wanted to give her hope that he was still alive. It seemed to comfort her. Maybe he's in Texas, they'd say. Or he's in the Rocky Mountains. Or even New York City.

His family apparently never contacted the police about Chris's disappearance. They did not file a missing person report. "They assumed I was off doing something on my own," said Chris. "Having an adventure. We Yankees, we see the world differently." Sergeant Hughes said he wasn't particularly surprised to learn that the Knights had not involved the authorities. "They're a rural Maine family," he said. "Keep-to-themselves people."

As a young boy, when the lilacs bloomed, Chris would gather a bouquet and give them to his mother. "I like the odor and the color, and it's one of the first flowers in spring. I remember thinking I'd found something new," he said. Otherwise there were few overt expressions of love. "We didn't feel the need to communicate everything all the time," Chris continued. "We're not emotionally bleeding all over each other. We're not touchy-feely. We weren't in the habit of being physically demonstrative. In my family, the boys could not express feelings. We relied on unspoken understandings. It was the way it was."

People who knew Chris as a child called him "quiet" and "shy" and "nerdy," but no one detected any deeper malaise. "I didn't find him to be all that weird," said Jeff Young, who went to elementary school, junior high, and high school with Chris and often rode the bus with him. "He was a wicked smart kid, and he had a really good sense of humor." Knight could also be silly and mischievous in a high school sort of way. Young recalled that when they took driver's education classes together, one time Chris deliberately drifted too close to the side of the road, rubbing the car against some bushes. It had recently rained, and the instructor, in the passenger seat with the window open, got drenched.

The Knight family never went skiing; they did not eat lobster. "Not our socioeconomics," said Chris. They owned snowshoes—"the long wooden ones, with the bear-claw bindings"—and they fished the local rivers with live bait. In winter, the family would head up to a relative's hunting camp in the North Woods and the Knight boys would ride snow-mobiles until one or two o'clock in the morning.

Once, Chris went skydiving with his brother Joel. They listened to the instructions, took off in a small airplane, then jumped out. It was the only plane flight of Chris's life. "So I have taken off in a plane, but I have never landed in one. How amusing."

As the youngest son, Chris was, of course, ribbed by his older brothers. They bestowed upon him the pet name Fudd, perhaps after the cartoon character Elmer Fudd, rube to Bugs Bunny. Chris detested the name. His parents were strict—early curfews, finish your homework, no junk food. One cousin, Kevin Nelson, told the *Kennebec Journal* that he used to bicycle over to the Knights' house carrying treats for the boys. "They would lower a string from a bedroom window, and they'd raise a bag of snacks," Nelson said. "I don't believe they ever had soda pop."

Hunting was Sheldon's passion. His obituary in the *Morning Sentinel* contained a total of four words about his leisure time: "He enjoyed deer hunting." He kept a bearskin rug at the foot of his bed, from a black bear he had shot. Sometimes Chris joined his father on hunts. "A couple of hunting trips, I slept in the back of the pickup," he said, "but never alone and never in a tent. I slept in my bed in my family home, where my parents knew exactly where I was."

Chris was once a winner in the Maine moose-license lottery, a lucky chance. He was sixteen years old and went into the woods near the Canadian border with his father, who lent him a .270 Winchester bolt-action rifle. Chris shot a seven-hundred-and-fifty-pound female moose and field-dressed it himself. "I was quite proud. My license, my kill. We ate well that year."

At Lawrence High School, where his class had two hundred and twenty-four students, Chris felt "invisible." He attended no social events, played no sports, joined no clubs. He never went to a football game and he skipped the prom, though he did have, he said, "two or three" friends. His classmate Larry Stewart recalled spending a few evenings hanging out with Chris. "I remember one night in particular," said Stewart. "We were driving around in a guy's car, and Chris was in the backseat. We just did what kids do up in Maine—we didn't tip over any cows or anything, but maybe we snuck a few drinks out of someone's beer, or drove around the old Concourse listening to Foreigner and Aerosmith, and went to McDonald's or something. Chris was smart and friendly. I never noticed anything odd about him, but who knows what was really going on? Us Mainers, we have our own way of doing things. We like to hold our peacoats and our family really close."

One day, Chris and Jeff Young decided to skip school and

go fishing. "We planned it the day before," said Young, "and took our fishing rods to school. Just the two of us. I think he didn't like being around too many people, and I don't blame him. We walked two or three miles, heading to the old metal bridge over the Sebasticook River. We never made it." Sheldon must have suspected something, for he drove by in his red Dodge pickup. Chris had respect for his father, Young observed, and perhaps a little fear of him. Without saying a word, Chris just got in the truck and left.

During his senior year, Knight, like most Maine public school students, attended a course called Hunter Safety and Outdoor Skills. He learned things like how to read a compass and how to construct a makeshift shelter. "This is something that keeps replaying in my mind," said his teacher, Bruce Hillman. "I told every kid that if you are in a survival situation, life or death, and you come upon a camp, it's okay to break in. This is accepted in Maine. I have a camp, too, and I always leave dry goods behind just in case others need it. You never know what impact you're going to have on some kid. I was thinking of a survival situation lasting two or three days, not twenty years."

The early 1980s brought the first generation of personal computers, and Knight was fascinated—one might expect him to be a technophobe, but he was actually an early adopter. His future plan, according to the yearbook, was to be a "computer technician." (His nickname, unsatisfyingly, was "Knight.") His favorite subject was history.

"I hated gym," he said. "I hated gym teachers. What's that Woody Allen line? 'Those who can't do, teach. And those who can't teach, teach gym.' I figured out a way of skipping gym class by going to study hall instead, and I weaseled my way out of four years of high school gym. I'm in good shape, I'm above average height. I just didn't want to play on teams. Being in gym class made me feel like I was trapped in *Lord of the Flies*. Can you really expect to see me playing volleyball?"

Upon graduation, Knight enrolled in a nine-month electronics course, whose curriculum included computer repair, at Sylvania Technical School in Waltham, Massachusetts, outside Boston. Two of his brothers had taken the same course. After he finished, he stayed in Waltham, where he found a job installing home and vehicle alarm systems, useful knowledge to have for his later career as a burglar. He rented a room in a house and purchased a new vehicle, a white 1985 Subaru Brat. His brother Joel co-signed the loan. "He did such a nice thing for me, and I screwed him on that," Knight said. "I still owe him."

He worked for less than a year, and then suddenly, without giving notice to his boss, quit the alarm-installation job. Knight never even returned his work tools, according to Kerry Vigue, the longtime family friend. His employer, irate, contacted Chris's family and demanded several hundred dollars in reimbursement for the missing tools, threatening legal action if they refused. Chris's parents, recalled Vigue, ended up paying.

Chris, meanwhile, cashed his final paycheck and left town. He did not tell anyone where he was going. "I had no one to tell," he said. "I didn't have any friends. I had no interest in my co-workers." He drove the Brat south. He was twenty years old. He ate fast food and stayed in cheap motels—"the cheapest I could find"—and drove for days, alone, until he found himself deep into Florida. He did not mention stopping at any tourist sites, or museums, or beaches. He stuck mostly to the interstate, and apparently didn't do much except sit in his car and watch the world, sealed off behind metal and glass. Eventually, he turned around and headed north. He listened to the radio. Ronald Reagan was president; the Chernobyl nuclear disaster had just occurred.

Something happened to Chris on that drive, the first and only road trip of his life. He headed north, through Georgia and the Carolinas and Virginia, blessed with the invincibility of youth, buzzed by "the pleasure of driving," and an idea grew into a realization, then solidified into a resolve. All his life, he'd been comfortable being alone. Interacting with others was so often frustrating. Every meeting with another person seemed like a collision. As he drove, perhaps he felt within himself some rumblings of fear and thrill, as if at the precipice of a radical leap.

He continued all the way back to Maine. There aren't many roads in the center of the state, and he chose the one that went right by his house. It wasn't a coincidence. "I think it was just to have one last look around, to say good-bye." He didn't stop. The last time he saw his family home was through the windshield of the Brat.

He kept going, "up and up and up." Soon he reached the shore of Moosehead Lake, the largest lake in Maine, where the state begins to get truly remote. "I drove until I was nearly out of gas. I took a small road. Then a small road off that small road. Then a trail off that." He went as far into wilderness as his vehicle could take him.

He parked the car and put the keys on the center console. He had a tent and a backpack but no compass, no map. Without knowing where he was going, with no particular place in mind, he stepped into the trees and walked away.

13

But why? Why would a twenty-year-old kid with a job and a car and a brain abruptly abandon the world? The act had elements of a suicide, except he didn't kill himself. "To the rest of the world, I ceased to exist," said Knight. His family must have suffered; they had no idea what had happened to him, and couldn't completely accept that he was dead. When his father died, fifteen years after the disappearance, Knight was still listed as a survivor in the obituary.

His final moment as a member of society—"I just tossed the keys on the center console"—seem particularly strange. Knight was raised with a keen appreciation for the value of money, and the Brat was the most expensive item he'd ever purchased. The car was less than a year old, and he threw it away. Why not hold on to the keys as a safety net? What if he didn't like camping out?

"The car was of no use to me. It had just about zero gas and was miles and miles from any gas station." As far as anyone knows, the Brat is still there, half-swallowed by the forest, a set of keys somewhere within, by this point as much a part of the wilderness as a product of civilization, perhaps like Knight himself.

Knight said that he didn't really know why he left. He'd given the question plenty of thought but had never arrived at an answer. "It's a mystery," he declared. There was no specific cause he could name—no childhood trauma, no sexual abuse. There wasn't alcoholism in his home, or violence. He wasn't trying to hide anything, to cover a wrongdoing, to evade confusion about his sexuality.

Anyway, none of these burdens typically produces a hermit. There's a sea of names for hermits—recluses, monks, misanthropes, ascetics, anchorites, swamis—yet no solid definitions or qualification standards, except the desire to be primarily alone. Some hermits have tolerated steady streams of visitors, or lived in cities, or holed up in university laboratories. But you can take virtually all the hermits in history and divide them into three general groups to explain why they hid: protesters, pilgrims, pursuers.

Protesters are hermits whose primary reason for leaving is hatred of what the world has become. Some cite wars as their motive, or environmental destruction, or crime or consumerism or poverty or wealth. These hermits often wonder how the rest of the world can be so blind, not to notice what we're doing to ourselves.

"I have become solitary," wrote the eighteenth-century French philosopher Jean-Jacques Rousseau, "because to me the most desolate solitude seems preferable to the society of wicked men which is nourished only in betrayals and hatred."

Across much of Chinese history, it was customary to protest a corrupt emperor by leaving society and moving into the mountainous interior of the country. People who withdrew often came from the upper classes and were highly educated. Hermit protesters were so esteemed in China that a few times, tradition holds, when a non-corrupt emperor was seeking a successor, he passed over members of his own family and selected a solitary. Most turned down the offer, having found peace in reclusion.

The first great literary work about solitude, the *Tao Te Ching,* was written in ancient China, likely in the sixth century B.C., by a protester hermit named Lao-tzu. The book's eighty-one short verses describe the pleasures of forsaking society and living in harmony with the seasons. The *Tao Te Ching* says that it is only through retreat rather than pursuit, through inaction rather than action, that we acquire wisdom. "Those with less become content," says the *Tao,* "those with more become confused." The poems, still widely read, have been hailed as a hermit manifesto for more than two thousand years.

Around a million protester hermits are living in Japan right now. They're called *hikikomori*—"pulling inward"—and the majority are males, aged late teens and up, who have rejected Japan's competitive, conformist, pressure-cooker culture. They have retreated into their childhood bedrooms and almost never emerge, in many cases for more than a decade. They pass the day reading or surfing the web. Their parents deliver meals to their doors, and psychologists offer them counseling online. The media has called them "the lost generation" and "the missing million."

Pilgrims—religious hermits—are by far the largest group. The connection between seclusion and spiritual awakening is profound. Jesus of Nazareth, after his baptism in the River Jordan, withdrew to the wilderness and lived alone for forty days, then began attracting his apostles. Siddhārtha Gautama, in about 450 B.C., according to one version of the story, sat beneath a pipal tree in India, meditated for forty-nine days, and became Buddha. Tradition holds that the prophet Muhammad, in A.D. 610, was on a retreat in a cave near Mecca when an angel revealed to him the first of many verses that would become the Koran.

In Hindu philosophy, everyone ideally matures into a hermit. Becoming a sadhu, renouncing all familial and material attachments and turning to ritual worship, is the fourth and final stage of life. Some sadhus file their own death certificates, as their lives are considered terminated and they are legally dead to the nation of India. There are at least four million sadhus in India today.

During the Middle Ages, after the Desert Fathers and Mothers of Egypt died out, a new form of Christian solitary emerged, this time in Europe. They were called anchorites—the name is derived from an ancient Greek word for "withdrawal"—and they lived alone in tiny dark cells, usually attached to the outer wall of a church. The ceremony initiating a new anchorite often included the last rites, and the cell's doorway was sometimes bricked over. Anchorites were expected to remain in their cells for the rest of their lives; in some cases, they did so for over forty years. This existence, they believed, would offer an intimate connection with God, and salvation. Servants delivered food and emptied chamber pots through a small opening.

Virtually every large town across France, Italy, Spain, Germany, England, and Greece had an anchorite. In many areas, there were more females than males. A woman's life in the Middle Ages was severely bound, and to become an anchorite, unburdened by social strictures or domestic toil, may have felt paradoxically emancipating. Scholars have called anchorites the progenitors of modern feminism.

Pursuers are the most modern type of hermits. Rather than fleeing society, like protesters, or living beholden to higher powers, like pilgrims, pursuers seek alone time for artistic freedom, scientific insight, or deeper self-understanding. Thoreau went to Walden to journey within, to explore "the private sea, the Atlantic and Pacific Ocean of one's being."

An endless list of writers and painters and philosophers and scientists have been described as hermits, including Charles Darwin, Thomas Edison, Emily Brontë, and Vincent van Gogh. Herman Melville, the author of *Moby-Dick,* largely withdrew from public life for thirty years. "All profound things," he wrote, "are preceded and attended by Silence." Flannery O'Connor rarely left her rural farm in Georgia. Albert Einstein referred to himself as a "loner in daily life."

The American essayist William Deresiewicz wrote that "no real excellence, personal or social, artistic, philosophical, scientific, or moral, can arise without solitude." The historian Edward Gibbon said that "solitude is the school of genius." Plato, Descartes, Kierkegaard, and Kafka have all been described as solitaries. "Not till we have lost the world," wrote Thoreau, "do we begin to find ourselves."

"Thoreau," said Chris Knight, offering his appraisal of the great transcendentalist, "was a dilettante."

Perhaps he was. Thoreau spent two years and two months, starting in 1845, at his cabin on Walden Pond in Massachusetts. He socialized in the town of Concord. He often dined with his mother. "I had more visitors while I lived in the woods than at any other period in my life," he wrote. One dinner party at his place numbered twenty guests.

While Knight lived in the woods, he didn't think of himself as a hermit—he never put a label on who he was—but when speaking of Thoreau, he used a particular phrase. Knight said that Thoreau was not a "true hermit."

Thoreau's biggest sin may have been publishing *Walden.* Knight said that writing a book, packaging one's thoughts into a commodity, is not something a true hermit would do. Nor is hosting a party or hobnobbing in town. These actions are directed outward, toward society. They all shout, in some way, "Here I am!"

Yet almost every hermit communicates with the outside world. Following the *Tao Te Ching,* so many protester hermits in China wrote poems—including poet-monks known as Cold Mountain, Pickup, Big Shield, and Stonehouse—that the genre was given its own name, *shan-shui.*

Saint Anthony was one of the first Desert Fathers, and the inspiration for thousands of Christian hermits who followed. Around A.D. 270, Anthony moved into an empty tomb in Egypt, where he stayed alone for more than a decade. He then lived in an abandoned fort for twenty years more, subsisting only on bread, salt, and water delivered by attendants, sleeping on the bare ground, never bathing, devoting his life to intense and often agonizing piety.

According to his biographer, Saint Athanasius of Alexandria, who met with him in person, Anthony ended his retreat with a pure soul and would go to heaven. But for much of his time in the desert, the biography adds, Anthony was inundated by parishioners seeking counsel. "The crowds," Anthony said, "do not permit me to be alone."

Even the anchorites, locked up by themselves for life, were not separate from medieval society. Their cells were often in town, and most had a window through which they counseled visitors. People realized that speaking with a sympathetic anchorite could be more soothing than praying to a remote and unflinching God. Anchorites gained widespread fame as sages, and for several centuries, much of the population of Europe discussed great matters of life and death with hermits.

In the forest, Knight never snapped a photo, had no guests over for dinner, and did not write a sentence. His back was fully turned to the world. None of the hermit categories fit him properly. There was no clear why. Something he couldn't quite feel had tugged him away from the world with the persistence of gravity. He was one of the longest-enduring solitaries, and among the most fervent as well. Christopher Knight was a true hermit.

"I can't explain my actions," he said. "I had no plans when I left, I wasn't thinking of anything. I just did it."

14

Knight actually did have a plan. Or maybe it was the opposite of a plan. Regardless, he had a goal: to get lost. Not just lost to the rest of the world but actually lost in the woods by himself. He carried only rudimentary camping supplies, a few articles of clothing, and a little food. "I had what I had," he said, "and nothing more." He left the keys in the car and vanished into the forest.

It's not that easy to get lost. Anyone with basic outdoor skills generally knows which way they're going. The sun burns west across the sky, and from there it's natural to set the other directions. Knight knew that he was heading south. He said he didn't make a conscious decision but felt pulled like a homing pigeon. "There was no depth or substance to the idea. It was at the instinctual level. It's instinct among animals to return to home territory, and my home ground, where I was born and raised, was that way."

Maine is partitioned into a series of long north-south valleys, the geologic clawmark left by glaciers surging and retreating. Separating the valleys are strings of mountains, now weather-worn and bald-topped like old men, but only a couple of dozen million years ago the Appalachians were mightier than the Rockies. The valley floors at the time of year when Knight arrived were a summer soup of ponds and wetlands and bogs.

"I kept largely to the ridges," Knight said, "and sometimes crossed swamps going from one ridge to another." He worked his way along crumbled slopes and muddy taiga. "Soon I lost track of where I was. I didn't care." Virtually every natural feature in Maine, pond to peak, has a proper name, but Knight saw such titles as human impositions and preferred not to know them. He sought a purity to his retreat beyond all measure. "There were no signs saying, 'You are here.' It was either dry land or wet land. I knew where I was but I didn't know where I was. Oh, I'm getting all metaphysical here, aren't I?"

He was unfettered by the rules of society, king of his own jungle, and alone and lost in the forest—a quilt of dreams and nightmares both. Knight mostly liked it. He'd camp in one spot for a week or so, then head south yet again. "I kept going," he said. "I was content in the choice I had made."

Content except for one thing: food. He was hungry, and he really didn't know how he'd feed himself. His departure was a confounding mix of incredible commitment and complete lack of forethought, not all that abnormal for a twenty-year-old. It was as if he went camping for the weekend and didn't come home for a quarter century. He was an able hunter and angler, but he carried neither a gun nor a rod. He didn't want to die, at least not then.

His idea was to "forage" for food. The wilds of Maine are enchanting to behold and monumentally broad, though not generous. There are no fruit trees. Berries sometimes have a weekend-long season. Without hunting or trapping or fishing, you're going to starve. Knight worked his way south, eating very little, until paved roads appeared. He found a road-killed partridge, but did not possess a stove or a way to easily start a fire, so he ate it raw. Neither a tasty meal nor a hearty one, and a good way to get sick.

He passed houses with gardens. Knight was raised with rigid morals and a great deal of pride. You make do on your own, always. No handouts or government assistance, ever. You know what's right and what's wrong, and the dividing line is usually clear.

But try not eating for ten days—nearly everyone's restraints will be eroded. Hunger is hard to ignore. "It took a while to overcome my scruples," Knight said, but as soon as his scruples fell, he snapped off a few ears of corn, dug up some potatoes, and ate a couple of green vegetables.

One time, during his first weeks away, he spent the night in an unoccupied cabin. It was a miserable experience. "The stress of that, the sleepless worry about getting caught, programmed me not to do that again." He never slept indoors after that, not once, no matter how cold or rainy the weather.

He continued moving south, picking through gardens, and eventually reached a region with a familiar distribution of trees, a diversity of birdcalls and bugs he recognized, and a temperature range he felt accustomed to. It had been colder up north. He wasn't sure precisely where he was, but he knew it was home ground. It turned out that he was less than thirty miles, as the crow flies, from his childhood home.

He came upon a pair of lakes, one large and one small, with cabins all around and plenty of small gardens offering easy snacking. Knight hoped to stay awhile, but there seemed to be no good place to camp, nothing offering both comfort and seclusion.

In the early days of his escape, nearly everything Knight learned was through trial and error, with the great hope that no error would end his seclusion. He had been gifted with a good head for figuring out workable solutions to complicated problems. All his skills, from the rigging of tarps to rainwater filtration to walking through the forest without leaving tracks, went through multiple versions and were never considered perfect. Tinkering with his systems was one of Knight's hobbies.

For a while, he tried living in a riverbank. The bank was tall and steep, and the stream offered a nice trickling soundscape. With a stolen shovel, Knight tunneled deep into the bank, reinforcing the walls and ceilings with scavenged wood, so that the dwelling resembled an old mine shaft. It wasn't acceptable. He was basically living in a hole, cold and damp, with hardly enough room to sit up. It was well camouflaged, but the forest around the cave offered far too easy walking. And, indeed, the spot was eventually discovered by deer hunters, long after Knight had abandoned it. The cave became a pilgrimage site for locals seeking answers to the hermit legend, though no one was sure if it had actually been constructed by him, or even if there was a hermit at all.

Knight tried at least six other places in the area, over a span of several months, without satisfaction. Finally he stumbled upon a region of nasty, boulder-choked woods without so much as a game trail running through it, far too harsh for hikers. He'd found the Jarsey, and he liked it immediately. Then he discovered the elephant rocks with the hidden opening. "I knew at once it was ideal. So I settled in."

He still remained hungry. He wanted more than vegetables, and even if he did stick with gardens, the Maine summer, as every local knows, is that rare lovely guest who leaves your house early. Once it ended, Knight understood, for the next eight months the gardens and cornfields would lay fallow beyond snacking.

Knight was realizing something almost every hermit in history has discovered: you can't actually live by yourself all the time. You need help. Hermits often end up in deserts and mountains and boreal woodlands, the sorts of places where it's nearly impossible to generate all your own food.

To feed themselves, several Desert Fathers wove reed baskets, which their assistants sold in town, using the proceeds to buy rations. In ancient China, hermits were shamans and herbalists and diviners. English hermits took jobs as toll collectors, beekeepers, woodcutters, and bookbinders. Many were beggars.

In eighteenth-century England, a fad swept the upper class. Several families felt their estate needed a hermit, and advertisements were placed in newspapers for "ornamental hermits" who were slack in grooming and willing to sleep in a cave. The job paid well, and hundreds of hermits were hired, typically on seven-year contracts, with one meal a day included. Some would emerge at dinner parties and greet guests. The English aristocracy of this period believed hermits radiated kindness and thoughtfulness, and for a couple of decades it was deemed worthy to keep one around.

Knight, of course, felt that anyone's willing assistance tainted the whole thing. Either you are hidden or you're not, no middle ground. He wished to be unconditionally alone, exiled to an island of his own creation, an uncontacted tribe of one. A single phone call letting his parents know he was okay and suddenly there would be a connection.

The cabins around the ponds, Knight noted, had minimal security measures. Windows were often left open, even when the owners were away. The woods offered excellent cover, and with few permanent residents, the area would soon be empty for the off-season. A summer camp with a big pantry was nearby. The easiest way to become a hunter-gatherer here was obvious.

And so Knight came to a conclusion. He decided to steal.

15

To commit a thousand break-ins before getting caught, a world-class streak, requires precision and patience and daring and luck. It also demands a specific understanding of people. "I looked for patterns," Knight said. "Everyone has patterns." Knight perched at the edge of the woods and meticulously observed the families of North Pond, quiet breakfasts to dinner parties, visitors to vacancies, cars up and down the road, like some Jane Goodall of the human race. Nothing he saw tempted him to return.

He wasn't a voyeur, he insisted. His surveillance was clinical, informational, mathematical. He did not learn anyone's name. All he sought was to understand migration patterns—when people went shopping, when a cabin was unoccupied. He watched the families move about and knew when he could steal.

After that, he said, everything in his life became a matter of timing. The ideal time to steal was deep in the night, midweek, preferably when it was overcast, best in the rain. A heavy downpour was prime. People stayed out of the woods when it was nasty, and Knight wished to avoid encounters. Still, he did not walk on roads or trails, just in case, and he never launched a raid on a Friday or Saturday, days he knew had arrived from the obvious surge in lakeside noise.

A constant dilemma was the "moon question." For a while, he opted to go out when the moon was large, so he could use it as a light source and have little need for a flashlight. In later years, when he suspected the police had intensified their search for him and he'd memorized much of the forest, he switched to no moon at all, preferring the cover of darkness. He liked to vary his methods, and he even varied how often he varied them. He didn't want to develop any patterns of his own, though he did make it a habit to embark on a raid only when freshly shaved or with a neatly groomed beard, and wearing clean clothing, to reduce suspicion on the slight chance that he was spotted.

There were at least a hundred cabins in Knight's repertoire—"one hundred might be a low number"—in addition to the providential Pine Tree kitchen, and he continually shuffled the ones he broke into. The ideal was a fully stocked place, with the family away until the weekend. He knew, in many cases, the precise number of steps required to reach a particular cabin, and once he selected a target, he bounded and wove through the forest, a touch of Tarzan to his style. "I have woodscraft," Knight acknowledged, choosing an elegant term.

Sometimes, if he was headed far or needed a load of propane or a replacement mattress—his occasionally grew moldy—it was easier to travel by canoe. He never stole one.

Canoes are difficult to hide, and if you steal one, the owner will call the police. It was wiser to borrow; there was a large selection around the lake, some up on sawhorses and seldom used. Almost no one calls the authorities if they suspect their canoe has been borrowed and returned undamaged.

Knight was capable of reaching homes anywhere on the two ponds. "I'd think nothing of paddling for hours, whatever needed to be done." If the water was choppy, he'd place a few rocks in the front to keep the boat stable. He'd typically stick close to shore, cloaked against the trees, hiding in the silhouette of the land, though once in a while, on a stormy night, he'd paddle across the middle, alone in the dark and lashed by the rain.

When he arrived at his chosen cabin, he'd make sure there were no vehicles in the driveway, no sign of someone inside—all the obvious things. This wasn't sufficient. Burglary is a dicey enterprise, a felony offense, with a low margin for error. One mistake and the outside world would snatch him back. So he crouched in the dark and waited.

Two hours, three hours, four hours, more. He needed to be sure no one was nearby, no one was watching, no one had called the police. This was not difficult for him; patience is his forte. "I enjoy being in the dark. Camouflage is my instinct. My favorite colors are those that helped me blend in. Dark green a shade darker than John Deere green is my favorite color." He never risked breaking into a home occupied year-round—too many variables—and he always wore a watch so he could monitor the time. Knight, like a vampire, did not want to stay out past sunrise.

Sometimes, especially in the early years, a few cabins were left unlocked. Those were the easiest to enter, though soon other places, and later the Pine Tree freezer, became nearly as simple—Knight had keys to them, ones he'd found during previous break-ins. Rather than travel around with a big jangling key chain, he stashed each key on its property, typically under some nondescript rock. He created several dozen of these stashes and never forgot where one was.

He noticed when several cabins left out pens and paper, requesting a shopping list, and others offered him bags of books, hanging from a doorknob. But he was fearful of traps, or tricks, or initiating any sort of correspondence, even a grocery list. So he left everything untouched, and the trend faded away.

For the majority of his break-ins, Knight worked the lock on a window or door. He always carried his lock-breaking kit, a gym bag with a collection of screwdrivers and flat bars and files, and he could defeat all but the most fortified bolts with the perfect little jiggle of just the right tool, less about muscle and more like Houdini.

If you had a really sophisticated door lock, he'd go in through a window. The idea of smashing glass or kicking down a door was appalling to Knight, the purview of barbarians. When he was finished stealing, he would often reseal the hasp on the window he'd unlatched and exit through the front door, making sure the handle was set, if possible, to lock up behind himself. No need to leave the place vulnerable to thieves.

As the residents of North Pond invested in security upgrades, Knight adapted. He knew about alarms from his one paying job, and he used this knowledge to continue stealing—sometimes disabling systems or removing memory cards from surveillance cameras, before they became smaller and better hidden.

He evaded dozens of attempts to catch him, by both police officers and private citizens. One time Sergeant Hughes served as driver for a search party that included officers from the state police. Everyone piled into the back of Hughes's four-wheel-drive truck, and they drove the rugged forest roads, stopping frequently to investigate on foot. "We searched and searched and never did find the hermit or his camp," said Hughes. With the vigilantes, including the man who spent more than a dozen nights lying in wait with his gun, Knight either sensed their presence or got a bit lucky.

The crime scenes themselves were so clean that the authorities offered their begrudging respect. "The level of discipline he showed while he broke into houses," said Hughes, "is beyond what any of us can remotely imagine—the legwork, the reconnaissance, the talent with locks, his ability to get in and out without being detected." A burglary report filed by one police officer specifically noted the crime's "unusual neatness." The hermit, many officers felt, was a master thief. It was as if he were showing off, picking locks yet stealing little, playing a strange sort of game.

Knight said that the moment he opened a lock and entered a home, he always felt a hot wave of shame. "Every time, I was very conscious that I was doing wrong. I took no pleasure in it, none at all."

Once inside a cabin, he moved purposefully, hitting the kitchen first before making a quick sweep of the house, looking for any useful items or the batteries he always required. He never turned on a light. He used only a small flashlight attached to a metal chain he wore around his neck—this style allowed him to leave the light dangling if he needed it in the forest, and it would illuminate only the ground, keeping his face shadowed. Knight detested headlamps; they scattered light everywhere, bright as a bar sign.

During a burglary, there wasn't a moment's ease. "My adrenaline was spiking, my heart rate was soaring. My blood pressure was high. I was always scared when stealing. Always. I wanted it over as quickly as possible." The only time he paused for more than a moment during a raid was when the weather was cold and he needed to thaw something out. If meat was frozen, he'd pop it in the microwave.

He'd finish with the inside of the cabin, then by habit check the gas grill to see if the propane tank was full. If so, and there was an empty spare lying around, he'd replace the full one with an empty, making the grill appear untouched. It was always best, Knight believed, for a home owner to have no clear evidence that he or she had been robbed. Then he'd load everything into a canoe, if it was a canoe-borrowing trip, and paddle to the shore closest to his camp and unload. He'd return the canoe to the spot he'd taken it from, sprinkle some pine needles on the boat to make it appear unused, then haul his loot up through the Jarsey, between the elephant rocks, to his site.

By this point, dawn was often breaking. When he carried

the last item into his camp, he could finally relax. "Ahead of me was a long stretch of peace. No, not peace. That's too icky of a word. A long stretch of calm." Each raid brought him enough supplies to last about two weeks, and as he settled once more into his room in the woods—"back in my safe place, success"—he came as close as he could to experiencing joy.

16

Knight lived in the dirt but was cleaner than you. Way cleaner. Pine needles and mud don't make you dirty, except superficially. The muck that matters, the bad bacteria, the evil virus, is typically passed through coughs and sneezes and handshakes and kisses. The price of sociability is sometimes our health. Knight quarantined himself from the human race and thus avoided our biohazards. He stayed phenomenally healthy. Though he suffered deeply at times, he insists he never once had a medical emergency, or a serious illness, or a bad accident, or even a cold.

During the summers, especially in the early years, he was strong, fit, and spry. "You should have seen me in my twenties—I ruled the land I walked upon, it was mine," Knight said, exposing the prideful streak that runs below his surface of contrition. "Why shouldn't I claim it as my own? No one else was there. I was in control. I controlled it as much as I wanted. I was lord of the woods."

Poison ivy grows throughout the area; its prevalence prevented some people from searching for his site. Knight kept a little jingle in his head—"leaves of three, let it be"—and so ably memorized where each patch grew that even at night he didn't brush against it. He says he was never once afflicted.

Lyme disease, a bacterial illness transmitted through tick bites that can cause partial paralysis, is endemic to central Maine, but Knight was spared that as well. He brooded about Lyme for a while, then came to a realization: "I couldn't do anything about it, so I stopped thinking about it."

Living in the woods, subject to the whims of nature, offers a great deal of autonomy but not much control. At first, Knight worried about everything: snowstorms might bury him, hikers could find him, the police would capture him. Gradually, methodically, he shed most of his anxiety.

But not all. Being too relaxed, he felt, was also a danger. In appropriate doses, worry was useful, possibly lifesaving. "I used worry to encourage thought," he said. "Worry can give you an extra prod to survive and plan. And I had to plan."

At the conclusion of each thieving mission, he was absolved temporarily of worry. The order in which he ate his food was governed by the pace of spoilage, ground beef to Twinkies. When he was down to little more than flour and shortening, he'd mix those together with water and make biscuits. He never stole homemade meals or unwrapped items, for fear someone might poison him, so everything he took came sealed in a carton or can. He ate every morsel, scraping the containers clean. Then he deposited the wrappers and cartons in his camp's dump, stuffed between boulders at the boundary of his site.

The dump was scattered over an area of about a hundred

square feet. One section was devoted to items like propane tanks and old mattresses and sleeping bags and books, another to food containers. Even in the food area, there was no odor. Knight added layers of dirt and leaves to aid with composting, which eliminated any smell, but most of the packaging was waxed cardboard or plastic, slow to disintegrate. Upon excavation, the colors on many boxes remained garish, superlatives and exclamation points and rococo typography popping from the soil while robins chirped in the branches above.

The archeological record contained in his dump revealed why Knight's only significant health issue was his teeth. He brushed regularly, he stole toothpaste, but did not see a dentist and his teeth began to rot. It didn't help that his culinary preferences never progressed beyond the sugar-and-processed-food palate of a teenager. "'Cooking' is too kind a word for what I did," he said.

A staple meal was macaroni and cheese. Dozens of mac-and-cheese boxes were buried between the rocks, along with several empty spice bottles—black pepper, garlic powder, hot sauce, blackened seasoning. Often, when Knight was inside a cabin with a good spice rack, he would grab a new bottle and try it out on his macaroni and cheese.

Also in his dump was a flattened thirty-ounce container from cheddar-flavored Goldfish crackers, a five-pound tub from Marshmallow Fluff, and a box that had held sixteen Drake's Devil Dogs. There were packages from graham crackers, tater tots, baked beans, shredded cheese, hot dogs, maple syrup, chocolate bars, cookie dough. Betty Crocker scalloped potatoes and Tyson chicken strips. Country Time lemonade and Mountain Dew. El Monterey spicy jalapeño and cheese chimichangas.

All of this came from a single kitchen-sink-sized hole, dug out by hand. Knight had fled the modern world only to live off the fat of it. The food, Knight pointed out, wasn't exactly his choice. It was first selected by the cabin owners of North Pond, then snatched by him. He did steal a little money, an average of fifteen dollars a year—"a backup system," he called it—and lived an hour's walk from the Sweet Dreams convenience store and deli, but never went there. The last time he ate at a restaurant, or even sat at a table, was at some fast-food place during his final road trip.

He stole frozen lasagna, canned ravioli, and Thousand Island dressing. You can dig in the dump until you're lying on your side, arm buried to the shoulder, and more keeps emerging. Cheetos and bratwurst and pudding and pickles. Quarry a trench deep enough to fight a war from—Crystal Light, Cool Whip, Chock full o'Nuts, Coke—and you still won't reach bottom.

So he wasn't a gourmet. He didn't care what he ate. "The discipline I practiced in order to survive did away with cravings for specific food. As long as it was food, it was good enough." He spent no more than a few minutes preparing meals, yet he often passed the fortnight between raids without leaving camp, filling much of the time with chores, camp maintenance, hygiene, and entertainment.

His chief form of entertainment was reading. The last moments he was in a cabin were usually spent scanning bookshelves and nightstands. The life inside a book always felt welcoming to Knight. It pressed no demands on him, while the world of actual human interactions was so complex. Conversations between people can move like tennis games, swift and unpredictable. There are constant subtle visual and verbal cues, there's innuendo, sarcasm, body language, tone. Everyone occasionally fumbles an encounter, a victim of social clumsiness. It's part of being human.

To Knight, it all felt impossible. His engagement with the written word might have been the closest he could come to genuine human encounters. The stretch of days between thieving raids allowed him to tumble into the pages, and if he felt transported he could float in bookworld, undisturbed, for as long as he pleased.

The reading selection offered by the cabins was often dispiriting. With books, Knight did have specific desires and cravings—in some ways, reading material was more important to him than food—though when he was famished for words, he'd subsist on whatever the nightstands bestowed, highbrow or low.

He liked Shakespeare, *Julius Caesar* especially, that litany of betrayal and violence. He marveled at the poetry of Emily Dickinson, sensing her kindred spirit. For the last seventeen years of her life, Dickinson rarely left her home in Massachusetts and spoke to visitors only through a partly closed door. "Saying nothing," she wrote, "sometimes says the most."

Knight wished he'd been able to procure more poetry written by Edna St. Vincent Millay, a fellow native of Maine, born in the coastal village of Rockland in 1892. He quoted her best-known lines—"My candle burns at both ends / It will not last the night"—and then added, "I tried candles in my camp for a number of years. Not worth it to steal them."

If he were forced to select a favorite book, it might be *The Rise and Fall of the Third Reich,* by William Shirer. "It's concise," Knight said, a quick twelve hundred pages, "and impressive as any novel." He stole every book on military history he saw.

He pilfered a copy of *Ulysses,* but it was possibly the one book he did not finish. "What's the point of it? I suspect it was a bit of a joke by Joyce. He just kept his mouth shut as people read into it more than there was. Pseudo-intellectuals love to drop the name *Ulysses* as their favorite book. I refused to be intellectually bullied into finishing it."

Knight's disdain for Thoreau was bottomless—"he had no deep insight into nature"—but Ralph Waldo Emerson was acceptable. "People are to be taken in very small doses," wrote Emerson. "Nothing can bring you peace but yourself." Knight read the *Tao Te Ching* and felt a deep-rooted connection to the verses. "Good walking," says the *Tao,* "leaves no tracks."

Robert Frost received a thumbs-down—"I'm glad his reputation is starting to fade"—and Knight said that when he ran out of toilet paper, he sometimes tore pages from John Grisham novels. He mentioned that he didn't like Jack Kerouac either, but this wasn't quite true. "I don't like people who like Jack Kerouac," he clarified.

Knight stole portable radios and earbuds and tuned in daily, voices through the waves another kind of human presence. For a while he was fascinated by talk radio. He listened to a lot of Rush Limbaugh. "I didn't say I liked him. I said I listened to him." Knight's own politics were "conservative but not Republican." He added, perhaps unnecessarily, "I'm kind of an isolationist."

Later he got hooked on classical music—Brahms and Tchaikovsky, yes; Bach, no. "Bach is too pristine," he said. Bliss for him was Tchaikovsky's *The Queen of Spades*. But his undying passion was classic rock: the Who, AC/DC, Judas Priest, Led Zeppelin, Deep Purple, and, above all, Lynyrd Skynyrd. Nothing in all the world received higher praise from Knight than Lynyrd Skynyrd. "They will be playing Lynyrd Skynyrd songs in a thousand years," he proclaimed.

On one raid he stole a Panasonic black-and-white five-inch-diagonal television. This was why he needed so many car and boat batteries—to power the TV. Knight was adept at wiring batteries together, in series and parallel. He also carried off an antenna and hid it high in his treetops.

He said that everything shown on PBS was "carefully crafted for liberal baby boomers with college degrees," but the best thing he watched while in the woods was a PBS program, Ken Burns's documentary *The Civil War*. He was able to recite parts of the show verbatim. "I still remember Sullivan Ballou's letter to his wife," said Knight. "It brought tears to my eyes." Ballou, a major in the Union army, wrote to Sarah on July 14, 1861, and was killed at the First Battle of Bull Run before the letter was delivered. The note spoke of "unbounded love" for his children, and Ballou said his heart was attached to his wife's "with mighty cables that nothing but Omnipotence could break"—an expression of human connection that made Knight weep, even if he wasn't compelled to seek it himself.

Knight was aware of world events and politics, but he seldom had any reaction. Everything seemed to be happening far away. He burned through all his batteries after September 11, 2001, and never watched television again. "Car batteries were so heavy and difficult to steal anyway," he said. He repurposed the ones he had as anchor weights for guylines, and after he stole a radio that received television audio signals, he switched to listening to TV stations on the radio; "theater of the mind," he called it. *Seinfeld* and *Everybody Loves Raymond* were his television-on-the-radio favorites.

"I do have a sense of humor," Knight said. "I just don't like jokes. Freud said there's no such thing as a joke—a joke is an expression of veiled hostility." His favorite comedians were the Marx Brothers, the Three Stooges, and George Carlin. The last movie he saw in a theater was the 1984 comedy *Ghostbusters*.

He never bothered listening to sports; they bored him, every one of them. For news, there were five-minute updates at the top of the hour on WTOS, the Mountain of Pure Rock, out of Augusta. Also, he said, he sometimes listened to French news stations out of Quebec. He didn't speak French, but he understood most of it.

He liked handheld video games. His rule for stealing them was that they had to appear outdated; he didn't want to take a kid's new one. He'd be stealing those in a couple years anyway. He enjoyed Pokémon, Tetris, and Dig Dug. "I like games that require thought and strategy. No shoot-'em-ups. No mindless repetitive motion." Electronic Sudoku was great, and crossword puzzles in magazines were welcome challenges, but he never took a deck of cards to play solitaire, and he doesn't like chess. "Chess is too two-dimensional, too finite of a game."

He didn't create any sort of art—"I'm not that type of person"—nor did he spend any nights away from his camp. "I have no desire to travel. I read. That's my form of travel." He never even glimpsed Maine's celebrated coastline. He claimed that he did not speak to himself aloud, not a word. "Oh, you mean like typical hermit behavior, huh? No, never."

Not for a moment did he consider keeping a journal. He would never allow anyone to read his private thoughts; therefore, he did not risk writing them down. "I'd rather take it to my grave," he said. And anyway, when was a journal ever honest? "It either tells a lot of truths to cover a single lie," he said, "or a lot of lies to cover a single truth."

Knight's ability to hold a grudge was impressive. Though many *National Geographic* magazines were buried beneath his tent, he despised the publication. "I didn't even like stealing them," he said. "I only looked at them when I was desperate. They're really only good for burying in the dirt. That glossy paper lasts a long time."

His aversion to *National Geographic* extends back to his youth. When Knight was in high school, he was reading a copy and came across a photo of a young Peruvian shepherd standing beside a road, crying. Behind him were several dead sheep, struck by a car as the boy had been trying to guide them. The photograph was later reprinted in a book of *National Geographic*'s all-time greatest portraits.

It incensed Knight. "They published a photo of the boy's humiliation. He had failed his family, who had entrusted him with the herd. It's disgusting that everybody can see a little boy's failure." Knight, still furious about the image thirty years later, was a man acutely attuned to the ravages of shame. Had he done something shameful before he'd fled to the forest? He insisted that he had not.

Knight had a strong distaste for big cities, filled with helpless intellectuals, people with multiple degrees who couldn't change a car's oil. But, he added, it wasn't as if rural areas were Valhalla. "Don't glorify the country," he said, then tossed off a line from the first chapter of *The Communist Manifesto* about escaping "the idiocy of rural life."

He acknowledged, forthrightly, that a couple of cabins were enticing because of their subscriptions to *Playboy*. He was curious. He was only twenty years old when he disappeared, and had never been out on a date. He imagined that finding love was something like fishing. "Once I was in the woods, I had no contact, so there was no baited hook for me to bite upon. I'm a big fish uncaught."

One book that Knight never buried in his dump or packed away in a plastic tote—he kept it with him in his tent—was *Very Special People,* a collection of brief biographies of human oddities: the Elephant Man, General Tom Thumb, the Dog-Faced Boy, the Siamese twins Chang and Eng, and hundreds of sideshow performers. Knight himself often felt that he was something of circus freak, at least on the inside.

"If you're born a human oddity," says the introductory chapter of *Very Special People,* "every day of your life, starting in infancy, you are made aware that you are not as others are." When you get older, it continues, things are likely to get worse. "You may hide from the world," advises the book, "to avoid the punishment it inflicts on those who differ from the rest in mind or body."

There was one novel above all others, Knight said, that sparked in him the rare and unnerving sensation that the writer was reaching through time and speaking directly to him: Dostoyevsky's *Notes from the Underground*. "I recognize myself in the main character," he said, referring to the angry and misanthropic narrator, who has lived apart from all others for about twenty years. The book's opening lines are: "I am a sick man. I am a spiteful man. I am an unattractive man."

Knight also expressed no shortage of self-loathing, but it was offset by a fierce pride, as well as an occasional trace of superiority. So, too, with the unnamed narrator of *Underground*. On the final page of the book, the narrator drops all humbleness and says what he feels: "I have only in my life carried to an extreme what you have not dared to carry halfway, and what's more, you have taken your cowardice for good sense, and have found comfort in deceiving yourselves. So that perhaps, after all, there is more life in me than in you."

17

It wasn't reading or listening to the radio that actually occupied the majority of Knight's free time. Mostly what he did was nothing. He sat on his bucket or in his lawn chair in quiet contemplation. There was no chanting, no mantra, no lotus position. "Daydreaming," he termed it. "Meditation. Thinking about things. Thinking about whatever I wanted to think about."

He was never once bored. He wasn't sure, he said, that he even understood the concept of boredom. It applied only to people who felt they had to be doing something all the time, which from what he'd observed was most people. Hermits of ancient China had understood that *wu wei,* "non-doing," was an essential part of life, and Knight believes there isn't nearly enough nothing in the world anymore.

Knight's nothingness had another component. "Watching nature," he called it, but he wasn't satisfied with the description. "It sounds too Disneyfied." Nature, Knight clarified, is brutal. The weak do not survive, and neither do the strong. Life is a constant, merciless fight that everyone loses.

From his clearing in the woods, every sight line short, Knight heard far more than he saw, and over the years his hearing grew sharp. His existence had a seasonal sound track. Springtime brought wild turkeys—yelping hens, gobbling toms—as well as chirping frogs. "You can mistake them for crickets, but they're frogs." Summer hosted the songbird chorus, morning and evening performances, and a lake buzzing with powerboats, which to Knight was the quintessential sound of humans at play.

In autumn came the drumming of ruffed grouse, the birds beating their wings to attract mates, while deer moved over dry leaves as if "walking on cornflakes." In winter, the rumble of an ice crack propagating across one of the ponds sounded like a bowling ball rolling down an alley.

A heavy storm would blot out everything. After three or four days straight, Knight just got used to hearing the wind. Then when the wind stopped, it was silence that sounded like a stranger. Rain could fall torrentially, thunderbolts cracking with fury, and a really close lightning strike, Knight admitted, frightened him. "I like wet weather, but there's enough of the little boy in me that I don't like thunderstorms."

He saw plenty of deer some years, none other years. An occasional moose. Once, the hindquarters of a mountain lion. Never a bear. Rabbits were on a boom-or-bust cycle, a lot or a few. The mice were bold—they'd come into his tent while he was lying there and crawl on his boots. He never thought about keeping a pet: "I couldn't put myself in a situation where I'm competing with the pet for food and maybe have to eat the pet."

His closest companion may have been a mushroom. There are mushrooms all over Knight's woods, but this particular one, a shelf mushroom, jutted at knee height from the trunk of the largest hemlock in Knight's camp. He began observing the mushroom when its cap was no bigger than a watch face. It grew unhurriedly, wearing a Santa's hat of snow all winter, and eventually, after decades, expanded to the size of a dinner plate, striated with black and gray bands.

The mushroom meant something to him; one of the few concerns Knight had after his arrest was that the police officers who'd tromped through his camp had knocked it down. When he learned that the mushroom was still there, he was pleased.

Even in the warm months, Knight rarely left his camp during the daytime. The chief exception to this came at the tail end of each summer, as the cabin owners were departing and the mosquitoes died down, when Knight embarked on a brief hiking season. There were a couple of aesthetically pleasing groves he liked to visit, natural Zen gardens, one with a ghostly scatter of white birches with their paperlike bark, another with a breeze-triggered huddle of quaking aspens. He passed some time at a few sandbanks along the shore of North Pond that felt to him like tiny beaches. "Sometimes I'd stay up late," he said, "and listen to some crazy AM talk-radio show, and hike to a high clearing before dawn and watch the ground fog collect in the valley."

Fall foliage is undeniably beautiful, as easy to like as chocolate, but Knight felt that the woods were at their loveliest when the leaves were finished. He liked the skeletal look of bare branches. "I've read too much Victorian literature—old books, used, the ones with bookplates in them, and the plates always show bare-limbed trees, to convey a sense of loss or coming horror."

He never celebrated his birthday, or Christmas, or any human holiday; he was usually unaware of the exact date, unless he heard it on the radio. He periodically witnessed the northern lights, flowing in pinks and greens like billowing drapes hanging from the sky, and if a lunar eclipse was mentioned on the news, he walked to an open meadow and watched it. He could sense, by the flow of darkness and day, when the winter and summer solstices had arrived, as well as the autumnal and vernal equinoxes, though he marked the occasions with no special festivity. "I didn't sing, I didn't dance, I didn't make sacrifices."

Knight had a particular fondness for the days around the Fourth of July. He did not watch fireworks but instead enjoyed his own private show. "It was the peak of firefly season. I thought that was poetically appropriate. I suspect John Adams would approve. Wasn't it he who recommended fireworks on the Fourth of July?"

It seemed that Knight could immediately recall anything he had ever read or seen, though he insisted that he did not have a photographic memory. He just remembered it all. "Both Adams and Jefferson died on the Fourth of July in 1826," he added. He wondered if modern society, with its flood of information and tempest of noise, was only making us dumber. "I was not overwhelmed with data," he said. "I had a rather restricted diet, literally and figuratively." The internet, wrote

Nicholas Carr in *The Shallows,* his book about brain science and screen time, steadily chips away at one's "capacity for concentration and contemplation."

According to more than a dozen studies conducted around the world, Knight's camp—an oasis of natural quiet—may have been the ideal setting to encourage maximal brain function. These studies, examining the difference between living in a calm place and existing amid commotion, all arrived at the same conclusion: noise and distraction are toxic.

The chief problem with environmental noise one can't control is that it's impossible to ignore. The human body is designed to react to it. Sound waves vibrate a tiny chain of bones—the hammer, anvil, and stirrup, the old-time hardware store of the middle ear—and these physical vibrations are converted to electrical signals that are fired directly into the auditory cortex of the brain.

The body responds immediately, even during sleep. People who live in cities experience chronically elevated levels of stress hormones. These hormones, especially cortisol, increase one's blood pressure, contributing to heart disease and cellular damage. Noise harms your body and boils your brain. The word "noise" is derived from the Latin word *nausea.*

You don't need that much quiet to change things, or even have to be alone. But you do have to seek out a soothing environment, and you must do it often. Japanese researchers at Chiba University found that a daily fifteen-minute walk in the woods caused significant decreases in cortisol, along with a modest drop in blood pressure and heart rate. Physiologists believe our bodies relax in hushed natural surroundings because we evolved there; our senses matured in grasslands and woods, and remain calibrated to them.

A Duke regenerative biologist, Imke Kirste, working with mice, found that two hours of complete silence per day prompted cell development in the hippocampus, the brain region related to the formation of memory. Studies of humans in the United States, Great Britain, Holland, and Canada have shown that after passing time in quiet, rural settings, subjects were calmer and more perceptive, less depressed and anxious, with improved cognition and a stronger memory. Time amid the silence of nature, in other words, makes you smarter.

For Knight, the quintessence of serenity was a late-summer heat wave in midweek, when nearly every cabin was unoccupied. This happened maybe once a year. Then, deep in the night, he'd leave his camp and walk until the trees abruptly ended and the waters of the pond swayed before him. He'd drop his clothes and slip into the water. The lake's top few inches, after cooking all day in the sun, would be nearly bath warm. "I'd stretch out in the water," he said, "and lie flat on my back, and look at the stars."

18

The only book Knight didn't steal was the one he most often saw. "I had no need for a Bible," he said. Knight came from Protestant stock but did not attend church as a child, though he read every page of the Good Book. "I don't practice a religion. I can't claim a belief system. I would say at this point I'm more polytheist than monotheist. I believe there are multiple gods for multiple situations. I don't have names for these gods. But I do not particularly believe in one big god of all gods."

Instead, he affiliated himself with a school of thought. He practiced Stoicism, the Greek philosophy, descended from Socratic ideas, founded in the third century B.C. Stoics felt that self-control and harmonious existence with nature constituted a virtuous life, and that one must endure hardship without complaint. Passion must be subject to reason; emotions lead one astray. "There was no one to complain to in the woods, so I did not complain," Knight said.

In the absence of a deity, Knight seemed to have venerated Socrates. The philosopher, born in 469 B.C., was not himself a hermit but advocated the lifestyle. Socrates may have concluded that his most valuable possession was his leisure. "Beware the barrenness of a busy life" is a quote commonly attributed to him. He walked everywhere barefoot, and ate only the poorest quality meats. Nothing appeared to bother him. Socrates was sentenced to death, facilitated by a cup of hemlock tea, for impiety and heretical teaching. One becomes free, Socrates seems to have taught, not by fulfilling all desires but by eliminating desire.

When Knight faced life-threatening challenges in the forest, he chose not to express emotion, instead maintaining the dispassionate equanimity of a Stoic. At no point, he emphasized, did he pray to a higher power. With one exception. When the worst of a Maine winter struck, all rules were suspended. "Once you get below negative twenty, you purposely don't think. It's like there's no atheists in a foxhole. Same with negative twenty. That's when you do have religion. You do pray. You pray for warmth."

All of Knight's survival tactics were focused on winter. Each year, just as the cabins were shutting down for the season, often with food left behind in the pantry, Knight embarked on an intensified streak of all-night raids. "It was my busiest time. Harvest time. A very ancient instinct. Though not one usually associated with crime."

His first goal was to get fat. This was a life-or-death necessity. Every mammal in his forest, mouse to moose, had the same basic plan. He gorged himself on sugar and alcohol—it was the quickest way to gain weight, and he liked the feeling of inebriation. The bottles he stole were the signs of a man who'd never once, as he admitted, sat at a bar: Allen's Coffee Flavored Brandy, Seagram's Escapes Strawberry Daiquiri, Parrot Bay Coconut Rum, and something called Whipped Chocolate Valley Vines, a liquefied blend of chocolate, whipped cream, and red wine.

He filled plastic totes with nonperishable food. He took warm clothes and sleeping bags. And he stockpiled propane, hauling the potbellied white tanks from barbecue grills all around North and Little North Ponds. The tanks were vital—not for cooking (cold food still nourishes) or heat (burning gas in a tent can create enough carbon monoxide to kill you) but for melting snow to make drinking water. It was a fuel-intensive task; Knight required ten tanks per winter. When each tank was finished, he buried it near his site. He never returned an empty.

The supply-gathering process was a race against the weather. With the first significant snowfall of the season, typically in November, all operations shut down. It is impossible to move through snow without making tracks, and Knight was obsessive about not leaving a print. So for the next six months, until the spring thaw in April, he rarely strayed from his clearing in the woods. Ideally, he wouldn't depart from his camp at all the entire winter.

To combat the cold, Knight groomed his beard to winter length—about an inch: thick enough to insulate his face, thin enough to prevent ice buildup. For most of the summer, using stolen shaving cream, he'd remain clean-shaven, to stay cool, except during the height of mosquito season, when a heavy scruff served as a natural insect repellent. The blackflies can swarm so thickly in central Maine that you can't breathe without inhaling some; every forearm slap leaves your fingers sticky with your own blood. Many North Pond locals find peak insect season more challenging than the severest cold snap.

Once the bugs subsided, Knight would shave again, until the blustery season in late fall—facial hair also offers good protection from the wind. As for the hair on his head, he kept it simple: several times a year, he'd shave himself bald, using scissors and a disposable razor. While he lived in the woods, Knight never once appeared classically hermitlike, hirsute and disheveled, and only while he was in jail and no longer a hermit did he begin to look exactly like one. It was his idea of a practical joke.

It's natural to assume that Knight just slept all the time during the cold season, a human hibernation, but this is wrong. "It is dangerous to sleep too long in winter," he said. It was essential for him to know precisely how cold it was, his brain demanded it, so he always kept three thermometers in camp: one mercury, one digital, one spring-loaded. He couldn't trust just a single thermometer, and preferred a consensus.

When frigid weather descended, he went to sleep at seven-thirty p.m. He'd cocoon himself in multiple layers of sleeping bags and cinch a tie-down strap near his feet to prevent the covers from slipping off. If he needed to pee, it was too cumbersome to undo his bedding, so he used a wide-mouthed jug with a good lid. No matter what he tried, he couldn't keep his feet warm. "Thick socks. Multiple socks. Boot liners. Thin socks, thinking it was better to have my feet together, using the mitten theory. I never found a perfect solution." Still, he did not lose a toe or a finger to frostbite. Once in bed, he'd sleep six and a half hours, and arise at two a.m.

That way, at the depth of cold, he was awake. At extreme temperatures, it didn't matter how well wrapped he was—if he remained in bed much longer, condensation from his body could freeze his sleeping bag. His core temperature would plunge, and the paralyzing lethargy of an extreme chill would begin to creep over him, starting at his feet and hands, then moving like an invading army to his heart. "If you try and sleep through that kind of cold, you might never wake up."

The first thing he'd do at two a.m. was light his stove and start melting snow. To get his blood circulating, he'd walk the perimeter of his camp. "Out of the tent. Turn left. Fifteen paces. Turn left. Eight paces. To my winter toilet. Do my business. Twenty paces back. A big triangle. Around again. And again. I like to pace." He'd air out his sleeping bags, wicking away moisture. He did this every bitter-cold night for a quarter century. If it had snowed he'd shovel his site, pushing the snow to the camp's perimeter, where it accumulated in great frozen mounds, walling him in.

His feet never seemed to fully thaw, but as long as he had a fresh pair of socks, this wasn't really a problem. It is more important to be dry than warm. By dawn, he'd have his day's water supply. No matter how tempted he was to crawl back into his covers, he resisted. He had complete self-control. Naps were not permitted in his ideology, as they ruined his ability to achieve deep, rejuvenating sleep.

He sometimes felt disconcertingly exposed during winter. Few people were around, but with the leaves gone, the chances increased that his camp might be spotted. He had an alarm system—no one could walk silently in Knight's woods, except Knight, so there'd always be warning of an approach—and also an escape plan. If a person came near, Knight's idea was to avoid confrontation by moving deeper into the woods.

A short distance from his camp, Knight kept what he called his upper cache. Buried in the ground, so well camouflaged with twigs and leaves that you could walk right over it and never know, were two metal garbage bins and one plastic tote. They contained camping gear and winter clothes, enough so that if someone found his site, Knight could instantly abandon it and start anew. His commitment to isolation was absolute.

19

Knight was sensitive about being thought of as insane. "The idea of crazy has been attached to me," he acknowledged. "I understand I've made an unusual lifestyle choice. But the label 'crazy' bothers me. Annoys me. Because it prevents response." When someone asks if you're crazy, Knight lamented, you can either say yes, which makes you crazy, or you can say no, which makes you sound defensive, as if you fear that you really are crazy. There's no good answer.

If anything, Knight thought of himself, in the grand tradition of Stoicism, as the opposite of crazy—as entirely clearheaded and rational. When he learned that the bundles of magazines buried at his site were regarded by some locals as an eccentric habit, he was infuriated. Everything he did in the woods, he said, had a reason. "People don't comprehend the reasons. They only see craziness and absurdness. I had a strategy, a long-term plan. They don't comprehend because I'm not there to explain it." Those bundles were a sensible recycling of reading material into floorboards.

It's possible that Knight believed he was one of the few sane people left. He was confounded by the idea that passing the prime of your life in a cubicle, spending hours a day at a computer, in exchange for money, was considered acceptable, but relaxing in a tent in the woods was disturbed. Observing the trees was indolent; cutting them down was enterprising. What did Knight do for a living? He lived for a living.

Knight insisted that his escape should not be interpreted as a critique of modern life. "I wasn't consciously judging society or myself. I just chose a different path." Yet he'd seen enough of the world from his perch in the trees to be repulsed by the quantity of stuff people bought while the planet was casually poisoned, everyone hypnotized into apathy by "a bunch of candy-colored fluff" on a billion and one little screens. Knight observed modern life and recoiled from its banality.

Carl Jung said that only an introvert could see "the unfathomable stupidity of man." Friedrich Nietzsche wrote, "Wherever is the crowd is a common denominator of stench." Knight's best friend, Thoreau, believed that all societies, no matter how well intentioned, pervert their citizens. Sartre wrote, "Hell is other people."

Maybe the operative question, Knight implied, wasn't why someone would leave society but why anyone would want to stay. "The whole world is rushing headlong like a swelling torrent," a recluse once told Confucius. "Wouldn't you be better off following those who flee the world altogether?" The Indian writer Jiddu Krishnamurti has been quoted as saying, "It is no measure of health to be well adjusted to a profoundly sick society."

The Hermitary website, a digital storehouse of everything hermit-related, posted a series of essays by a modern solitude seeker—he described himself as a homeless wanderer—who used only the initial S. as a pen name. "Human society has been mostly an immoral violent bedlam," he wrote. There's an endless cycle of crime, corruption, disease, and environmental degradation. The answer to consumption is always more consumption, and society lacks any mechanism for finding a balance between humans and nature. At our core, we are really just beasts. S.'s conclusion was stark: "Living and participating in society *is* madness *and* criminal." Unless you are a hermit, in a state of permanent retreat from all others, he wrote, you are in some ways guilty of destroying the planet.

After his arrest, Knight was examined by a forensic psychologist hired by the state of Maine to evaluate his mental health. Court documents show that the state considered Knight to have "complete competency." The state also offered three diagnoses: Asperger's disorder, depression, or possible schizoid personality disorder.

No surprise with the Asperger's. For a while, every smart and shy eccentric from Bobby Fischer to Bill Gates was hastily fitted with this label, and many were more or less believably retrofitted, including Isaac Newton, Edgar Allan Poe, Michelangelo, and Virginia Woolf. Newton had great trouble forming friendships and probably remained celibate. In Poe's poem *Alone* he wrote that "all I lov'd—*I* lov'd alone." Michelangelo is said to have written, "I have no friends of any sort and I don't want any." Woolf killed herself.

Asperger's disorder, once considered a subtype of autism, was named after the Austrian pediatrician Hans Asperger, a pioneer, in the 1940s, in identifying and describing autism.

Unlike other early researchers, according to the neurologist and author Oliver Sacks, Asperger felt that autistic people could have beneficial talents, especially what he called a "particular originality of thought" that was often beautiful and pure, unfiltered by culture or discretion, unafraid to grasp at extremely unconventional ideas. Nearly every autistic person that Sacks observed appeared happiest when alone. The word "autism" is derived from *autos,* the Greek word for "self."

"The cure for Asperger's syndrome is very simple," wrote Tony Attwood, a psychologist and Asperger's expert who lives in Australia. The solution is to leave the person alone. "You cannot have a social deficit when you are alone. You cannot have a communication problem when you are alone. All the diagnostic criteria dissolve in solitude."

Officially, Asperger's disorder no longer exists as a diagnostic category. The diagnosis, having been inconsistently applied, was replaced, with clarified criteria, in the fifth edition of the *Diagnostic and Statistical Manual of Mental Disorders;* Asperger's is now grouped under the umbrella term autism spectrum disorder, or ASD.

It was unclear if Knight really did have ASD. A half dozen autism experts and clinical psychologists reviewed Knight's story. All of them said that it was impossible to make an accurate diagnosis without meeting the patient, but they agreed to comment. Thomas W. Frazier, the director of the Center for Autism at the Cleveland Clinic, felt it was "pretty obvious" that Knight had autisic traits, especially his lack of eye contact, his sensory touchiness, and his absence of friends. Autism has a genetic component, and Knight's family, so private and quiet, could possess what's known as a broad autism phenotype.

The South African neuroscientist Henry Markram, whose son is on the autism spectrum, has explained the disorder with what he calls the "intense world" theory—motions, sounds, and lights that most of us naturally disregard feel to an autistic person like an endless assault, their life a permanent visit to Times Square. Autistic people take in too much and learn too fast, overwhelmed not only by their own emotions but by the emotions of others. Looking at a person's face is like staring at a strobe light; a squeaky bedspring could sound like fingernails scraping across a blackboard. To remain stable, Markram believed, you'd have to regulate your life to the fullest extent possible, developing a rigorous focus on detail and repetition.

Oliver Sacks wrote that autistic people, as an adaptation to an "uninhibited barrage of sensation," often needed to create a world of their own, one that was calm and orderly. Some autistic people fashioned this world between their ears, but Knight built it amid the trees.

And yet according to Stephen M. Edelson, the executive director of the Autism Research Institute, in San Diego, Knight's behavior, however autistic-seeming, did not rise to the level of autism spectrum disorder. Edelson believed that given the opportunity to meet with Knight, few experienced doctors would deem him autistic. Knight's ability to plan and coordinate his life, to survive for so long completely on his own without therapy or treatment, is extremely uncharacteristic of an autistic person.

Catherine Lord, a professor of psychology at Weill Cornell Medicine, in New York, said that even the most autistic adult or child she'd ever encountered usually had someone in their lives they would like to be around. Many autistic people desire contact and hugs but don't know when it's appropriate. "For every autistic trait he has," said Peter Deri, a clinical psychologist in private practice in New York, "he has traits that are the antithesis. Autistic people don't steal. They're not criminals." Knight exhibited none of the repetitive movements or recurrent speech patterns typical of those with ASD.

Another idea proffered by the state psychologist who did examine Knight was schizoid personality disorder. This is not the same thing as schizophrenia, in which people characteristically lose contact with reality and often experience hallucinations and delusional thinking. Schizoid personality is similar to autism in that people with either disorder rarely have close relationships and tend to be logical thinkers. Those with autism, however, often want friends but find human social interaction too incomprehensible. People with schizoid personality disorder prefer to be solitary. They lack any general interest to be with others, even sexually. They know the social rules but have decided not to follow them; they are indifferent to everyone else. Jill Hooley, the head of the clinical psychology program at Harvard University, felt that Knight's behavior was consistent with many of the features of schizoid personality disorder.

There are good arguments why Knight both could and could not be diagnosed with schizoid personality disorder. The evidence showed that he was apathetic to people, in a schizoid way, but his inability to interact naturally with others and his hypersensitivity to sensory changes seemed classically autistic. "The temptation to label Knight is so great," said Peter Deri. "Was he depressed? Was he schizoid? Bipolar? Are there Aspergian traits?"

Maybe there's a brain abnormality—a damaged amygdala, a shortage of oxytocin, an imbalance of endorphins. Stephen M. Edelson suggested several syndromes before giving up and quipping, "I diagnose him as a hermit."

"Nothing makes complete sense," said Deri. "The complexity of this guy is so puzzling, you could go anywhere diagnostically. There has to be grandiosity to go through with a plan like that, it is so exceptional. Knight is like a Rorschach card. He really is an object for everyone to project onto."

Knight expressed little interest in his diagnosis. "I only learned about Asperger's here in jail. It's just a label slapped on a set of behaviors." He admitted that therapy might benefit him, but was adamant that any disorder assigned to him not be used as an excuse for his crimes. He said he was taking no medications.

"I don't want to be in the position of victim. It's not my nature. There's not much, from what I've read, that I can do about my diagnosis. I don't think I'll be a spokesman for the Asperger's telethon. Do they still do telethons? I hate Jerry Lewis."

20

The cabin owners of North Pond, a majority of them, arrived at a very different diagnosis. Knight was not just a thief, they said, but also a fraud.

"No way he's telling the truth," declared Fred King, who once had a sugar bowl stolen from his place, after which, for years, his friends called him Sugar Bowl. "Can I use a swear word?" asked King, gruff and polite at once, a very Maine trait. "There is no fucking way this guy was a hermit. I'm an outdoorsman, and I'm just telling you, flat out, no way. I'm a thousand percent sure. In winter, it's subzero all the time. I think a family member helped him, or another person took him in. Or he broke into a vacant place and stayed all winter."

Some people refused to accept that Knight had never once required medical care. Food stored in the woods, others noted, inevitably attracts raccoons and coyotes, which will tear your camp apart. And how was it possible, a couple of locals asked, that Knight could speak so well, that his vocal cords still functioned and he'd retained such an extensive vocabulary, if he really hadn't used his voice for so long? One resident pointed out that there was a road called Knight Court not far from his site, and a Knight family, likely relatives of Chris's, had lived there forever. They must have provided assistance. Also, if Knight had really been out there, the Great Ice Storm of 1998 would surely have frozen him.

"Everything that came from his camp stunk," said Steve Treadwell, the Pine Tree employee who'd observed the police interrogation of Knight and the dismantling of his site. "But he was clean-smelling. He didn't live in the woods. His story doesn't pass the smell test. Literally."

Dozens of North Pond summer residents offered their opinions about Knight, and about eighty percent of them insisted that he was lying, such an overwhelming preponderance that the only proper thing to do was ask Knight directly. Did he truly spend twenty-seven years alone in the woods? Or did he have assistance, or pass the winter in a cabin, or at least use someone's bathroom?

When questioned, Knight was adamant and a little angry. Other than the one time he stayed in a home, during the first few weeks of his escape, he never again slept inside. "I had no help from anybody, ever." He was not in touch with his family, he did not take a shower, nap in a bed, or lounge on someone's sofa even for a minute. The first time he used an actual toilet in a quarter century was in the Kennebec County jail. When he was driven to the jail in the back of a squad car, it was the first time he'd ridden in an automobile since abandoning the Brat. "I'm a thief. I induced fear. People have a right to be angry. But I have not lied."

Knight seemed entirely honest, practically incapable of

lying, a notion that several other people supported. Diane Vance said that much of her job as state trooper consisted of sorting through lies people fed her, but with Knight she had no questions. "Unequivocally," she said, "I believe him." Sergeant Hughes felt the same: "There's no doubt in my mind he's lived out there the whole time."

There was not a morsel of convincing evidence that Knight had ever spent an evening away from the woods, minus the one occasion he admitted to—an admission that itself was a sign of his precise honesty. He said he didn't need medical care because he wasn't exposed to germs. He kept his food sealed in plastic totes and remained in camp nearly all the time; most large animals won't approach when a human is present.

At the time of his arrest, after a long winter, he was down to a single set of unsoiled clothes—he was due for a laundry day. Even in the cold, he kept himself clean with sponge baths, preferably using a large yellow car-wash sponge, if he could steal one, and he frequently took shower gel and deodorant. He could speak so well because vocal cords do not, in fact, curl up and die with disuse, and speaking in complex sentences isn't about the mouth, it comes from the brain, which in Knight's case was fully operational, albeit idiosyncratic. Knight had no idea that a family of Knights lived nearby, and anyway they're not related; his surname is common in central Maine.

He wished there had been *more* Great Ice Storms. "Ice is nearly liquid. You don't have liquid in serious cold, in killing cold. It was twenty-eight degrees during that storm. In a car, driving, it was serious. For me, it was a novelty. Actually, it helped. It put a thick layer of ice over the snow, and I could walk around without leaving tracks."

Most of the North Pond locals, when they were informed that Knight's story was undoubtedly true, did not change their minds. They were convinced that Knight was running some bizarre con, and that all who believed him had fallen into his trap. They didn't reject his story mildly; they rejected it venomously. A few seemed less angry about having their goods stolen than the fact that Knight's tale was accepted by anyone. They couldn't get their heads around Knight. It was as if he'd insisted that he could flap his arms and fly. His story was both true and unbelievable at the same time, an unsettling merger.

The locals were rattled because Knight's feat went against all that felt natural, was antithetical to nearly everything one learns. In the Bible, in chapter 2 of Genesis, Adam's aloneness is the first thing God finds objectionable: "And the Lord God said, It is not good that the man should be alone."

One reason there are virtually no more devout Christian solitaries—and haven't been since the 1700s—is that they frightened the ecclesiastical authorities. Hermits were unsupervised thinkers, pondering life and death and God, and the church, with its ingrained schedules and rote memorization, did not approve of many hermits' ideas. Thomas Aquinas, the thirteenth-century Italian priest, said hermits could be subversive to obedience and stability, and that it was better to keep such people in monasteries, subject to regulations and routine.

"The solitary is necessarily a man who does what he wants to do," wrote Thomas Merton, an American Trappist monk who died in 1968. "In fact, he has nothing else to do. That is why his vocation is both dangerous and despised."

I began asking cabin owners—and, later, many others—to estimate the longest time they'd ever spent without human interaction. By this I meant not seeing anyone or communicating in any way, including phone, e-mail, or text messages. Just time by one's self, unconnected, though reading or listening to the radio or watching TV alone was okay.

Nine out of ten people, often after a contemplative pause, realized that they had never passed a single day in solitude. Usually it was no more than a handful of waking hours. My father has lived seventy-three years but hasn't tried a dozen hours alone. I once embarked on a three-day solo wilderness trip but encountered a pair of hikers and stopped to chat, so my record is around forty-eight hours. A few accomplished explorers I know have gone a week. To meet someone who's finished a month would be extraordinary.

Chris Knight, with his thousands upon thousands of days alone, was an unfathomable outlier. His feat goes so far beyond anyone else's physical or mental limit that it rearranges our notion of the possible. But the truth is that Knight was out there every one of those winters, and what he did in the cold was both prosaic and profound.

He suffered. When he ran out of propane and food, he often became "cold, cold, really cold." Such cold is often called mind-numbing, but he was aware of it always. He called it "physical, emotional, psychological pain." His body fat was eaten from within, his stomach begged. He sensed the nearness of death. Yet he refused to light a fire or leave a traceable footprint.

When the situation passed some point of dire, he monitored the weather reports on the radio and waited for a snowstorm to approach. With the exception of a few year-round homes, which Knight never touched, the area was mostly deserted in winter, and he knew which seasonal cabins likely still had food. With the last of his energy he'd slog through the forest, cut across the frozen pond, hit one of these cabins, and return as the flakes started to fall, erasing his tracks.

He could not always maintain an impassive neutrality. Sometimes a tiny thing wormed into the deep spot where he'd stashed his emotions. Once, as he was listening to the radio, a blizzard swirling around him, the school closures were announced. His old high school was mentioned. Just a moment on the radio, but it brought back a flood of memories. And Knight felt his chest clench with melancholy. How had his life come to this?

He occasionally missed his family. "I suppose a more subtle answer would be I missed some of my family to a certain degree," he allowed. For long stretches, family didn't exist in his thoughts. Then a memory would be triggered and they'd be alive in his head. He missed his sister, Susanna, the most. She's the sibling closest in age to Knight, a year younger, and has Down syndrome. "She was the one I spent most of my childhood with," he said.

There were times, he admitted, when he wept, but he provided no further details. Sporadically, especially during the first decade, the idea of quitting his seclusion entered his mind. He had a system in place. He kept a whistle in his tent, and if he ever became too weak to move, he knew that if he blew on it in sustained sequences of three, the high-pitched sounds would carry across the water and help might eventually come.

After a while, though, he resolved that he wouldn't use the whistle. He made a firm decision that he was not going to voluntarily emerge from the trees. Civilization was three minutes away, but he never went except to steal. "I was prepared to die out there," he said.

21

A thousand poets sing of solitude—"let me live, unseen, unknown," yearned Alexander Pope—but far more people curse it. The difference between bliss and distress generally seems to be whether solitude is chosen or involuntary. Forced isolation is one of the oldest known punishments. Banishment was widely used during the Roman Empire (the poet Ovid was exiled from Rome in A.D. 8, possibly for writing obscene verse), and for centuries a severe penalty on the high seas was marooning, in which an offending sailor was deposited on an uninhabited island, sometimes with a Bible and a bottle of rum. Most such men were never heard from again. Even now, when a Jehovah's Witness is disfellowshipped for breaking church doctrine, every member of the religion is forbidden from speaking to the sinner.

The worst nonlethal punishment in the United States penal system is solitary confinement. It's a "hell all to yourself," said Robert Stark, who has spent years in solitary at the Louisiana State Penitentiary, serving time for murder. Thomas Silverstein killed a prison guard in 1983 and since then (except for one week during a prison riot) has been locked alone in a concrete and steel box, during which he has never once felt an affectionate touch. It feels as if he's been "buried alive," Silverstein wrote, "for an entire lifetime."

Todd Ashker, who was isolated in a windowless supermax cell for about twenty-five years, described his situation as "a continuous silent screaming." John Catanzarite spent nearly fourteen years in solitary in a California prison and said that when he started to lose his sanity he was glad, because it might release him from the horror of reality.

After ten days in solitary confinement, many prisoners display clear signs of mental harm, and one study showed that about a third will eventually develop active psychosis. There are at least eighty thousand such inmates in America. The United Nations has determined that holding a person in isolation for more than fifteen days is cruel and inhuman punishment.

"It's an awful thing, solitary," wrote John McCain, who spent more than five years as a prisoner of war in Vietnam, two of them alone, before he became a U.S. senator. "It crushes your spirit," McCain added. "The onset of despair is immediate." A large majority of men, and twenty-five percent of women, a University of Virginia study found, would rather subject themselves to mild electric shocks than do nothing but sit quietly with their thoughts for fifteen minutes. Unless you are a trained meditator, the study's authors concluded, the "mind does not like to be alone with itself." Terry Anderson, kidnapped in Lebanon in 1985 and held mostly alone for more than six years, said, "I would rather have had the worst companion than no companion at all."

Many evolutionary biologists believe that early humans thrived, despite being weaker and slower than other animals, chiefly due to their superior ability to work together. Human brains are wired to connect—magnetic resonance imaging shows that the same neural circuitry that causes us to feel physical pain is activated when we face social pain, like being shunned from a group or picked last on the playground.

Harry Harlow, a psychology professor at the University of Wisconsin, ran a series of experiments starting in the 1950s, showing that young rhesus monkeys, when isolated from other monkeys for as little as three months, could be behaviorally damaged for life. Brain scans of war prisoners in the former Yugoslavia demonstrated that without sustained social interaction, a brain can become as injured as one that has incurred a traumatic blow. Upon being taken captive, John McCain had two broken arms and a broken leg, and later developed chronic dysentery, but the pain of loneliness, he implied, was worse.

Our inherent and environmentally stimulated sociability may have made our brains grow so large in the first place. "Reading and interpreting social cues," noted social neuroscientist John Cacioppo, "is, for any of us, at any time, a demanding and cognitively complex activity." The need to recognize the constantly shifting status of friends and foes, to act for the betterment of a group when it isn't in your immediate self-interest, to understand how to reason and cajole and deceive, likely gave rise to an expanded cerebral cortex, which, in turn, resulted in the dominance of humans.

Further, evolution selected genes that reinforce pleasure

and safety in company, and unease and fear when alone. Unwanted loneliness makes you sick—social isolation is as damaging as high blood pressure, obesity, or smoking as a risk factor for illness and early death. "Happiness for a member of the human species demands connection," wrote Cacioppo. "Our brains and bodies are designed to function in aggregates, not in isolation."

Connectivity and cooperation transcend humans; these traits extend to the most ancient forms of life. Many animals display extreme devotion to group bonding and social good. There are hives, flocks, herds, schools, gaggles, troops, packs, bands, bevies, coveys, and droves. (There are also lone wolves and solitary apes and even hermitlike wasps, but these are exceptions to the general rule of the animal kingdom.) *Salmonella* bacteria work together, secreting signaling molecules that help them determine the opportune moment to collectively attack a host. By the time a human infant is eight months old, attachments to others have already been formed. It's only Knight, and his fellow solitaries throughout history, who are puzzling anomalies.

After his arrest and incarceration, Knight craved solitary confinement. "I have a hope, wish, fantasy of a cell of my own," he wrote in one of his letters. "And to think this would be considered punishment. It is to laugh." But not aloud— Knight always made sure to laugh silently, internally. He worried that if he were seen grinning in jail, amused by a thought in his head, it would be considered further proof of his feeblemindedness.

For his first several months in jail, Knight had a cellmate, with whom he scarcely exchanged a word. When he was finally transferred to a single cell, he was much relieved.

Isolation is the raw material of greatness; being alone is hazardous to our health. Few other conditions produce such diametrically opposing reactions, though of course genius and craziness often share a fence line. Sometimes even voluntary solitude can send a person over to the wrong side of the fence.

In 1988, a cave explorer named Véronique Le Guen volunteered for an extreme experiment: to live alone in an underground cavern in southern France without a clock for one hundred and eleven days, monitored by scientists who wished to study the human body's natural rhythms in the absence of time cues. For a while, she settled into a pattern of thirty hours awake and twenty hours asleep. She described herself as being "psychologically completely out of phase, where I no longer know what my values are or what is my purpose in life."

When she returned to society, her husband later noted, she seemed to have an emptiness inside her that she was unable to fully express. "While I was alone in my cave I was my own judge," she said. "You are your own most severe judge. You must never lie or all is lost. The strongest sentiment I brought out of the cave is that in my life I will never tolerate lying." A little more than a year later, Le Guen swallowed an overdose of barbiturates and lay down in her car in Paris, a suicide at age thirty-three. "It was a risk that came with this experiment, to become half crazy," she'd reportedly said on a radio show two days earlier.

The first solo around-the-world sailing race, the Golden Globe, began in 1968. Bernard Moitessier of France was on his way to winning when he realized that he loved being alone on his boat and dreaded returning to the hubbub of society. He quit the race after seven months and continued sailing for nearly a complete second lap of the world, achieving a personal victory he found far more meaningful than any contest. "I am free, free as never before," he wrote.

But another competitor in the Golden Globe, Donald Crowhurst of Great Britain, became increasingly lonely and depressed, began radioing false reports about his progress, and finally retreated to his cabin, where he composed a lengthy and hallucinatory treatise. Then he went overboard. His body was never recovered. "It is finished. It is finished. It is the mercy" were some of his final written words.

The same solitude, that of the enormous emptiness of the ocean, moved Moitessier to ecstasy and drove Crowhurst to insanity. Knight had within him, it seemed, a little of both sailors—a dark side and a light, a yin of winter and a yang of summer. "Pain and pleasure," he called it. Both were essential, he believed, and one could not exist without the other. "Suffering is such a deep part of living," wrote Robert Kull, who lived alone on an island in Patagonia for a year, in 2001, "that if we try too hard to avoid it, we end up avoiding life entirely." The *Tao Te Ching* says that "happiness rests in misery."

"Man is sometimes extraordinarily, passionately, in love with suffering," wrote Dostoyevsky in *Notes from the Underground*. "Suffering is the sole origin of consciousness."

Jill Hooley, the Harvard psychology professor who felt that Knight's behavior displayed characteristics of schizoid personality disorder, observed that torment was the price Knight paid in order to remain in the woods. He was afflicted by cold and hunger, by fear during each break-in, by the guilt of knowing that what he was doing was wrong. His very existence was threatened throughout the winter. "It's an incredibly steep price to pay," said Hooley, "but he was clearly willing to pay it." However acute, his distress was preferable to the alternative: returning to society. Therefore, Hooley concluded, Knight must have received some tremendous benefit for himself, psychologically, from being separated from the world.

Many of Knight's most cherished and intense experiences in the woods, he said, were close to his most horrific. In the dead of winter, there was not a rustling leaf, not a candle flick of wind, not a bug or bird. The forest was locked in arctic silence. This was what he craved.

"What I miss most in the woods," Knight said, "is somewhere in between quiet and solitude. What I miss most is stillness." To reach this pristine state, the forest hard-frozen and the animals bunkered, he had to bring himself to the brink of death.

It was only when he heard the song of the chickadees, the state bird of Maine, that he knew winter would soon loosen its grip, "that the end was near." The feeling, he said, was momentous; he referred to it as a celebration, the chirps volleying through the trees, the little birds with their black-capped heads bobbing in the bare branches, calling their own names—*chick-a-dee-dee*—the sound of months of mute suffering coming to a close, the sound of survival. If he still had some fat left on his body, he was proud. Most times, he did not. "After a bad winter," Knight said, "all I could think was that I'm alive."

22

Snow melted, flowers bloomed, insects droned, deer bred. Years passed, or minutes. "I lost grasp of time," Knight said. "Years were meaningless. I measured time by the season and moon. The moon was the minute hand, the seasons the hour hand." Thunder cracked, ducks flew, squirrels gathered, snow fell.

Knight said that he couldn't accurately describe what it felt like to spend such an immense period of time alone. Silence does not translate into words. And he feared that if he tried a translation, he'd come across as a fool. "Or even worse, as spouting off phony wisdom or little koans." Thomas Merton, the Trappist monk, wrote that nothing can be expressed about solitude "that has not already been said better by the wind in the pine trees."

What happened to him in the woods, Knight claimed, was inexplicable. But he agreed to set aside his fear of phony wisdom and koans and give it a try. "It's complicated," he said. "Solitude bestows an increase in something valuable. I can't dismiss that idea. Solitude increased my perception. But here's the tricky thing: when I applied my increased perception to myself, I lost my identity. There was no audience, no one to perform for. There was no need to define myself. I became irrelevant."

The dividing line between himself and the forest, Knight said, seemed to dissolve. His isolation felt more like a communion. "My desires dropped away. I didn't long for anything. I didn't even have a name. To put it romantically, I was completely free."

Virtually everyone who has written about deep solitude has said some version of the same thing. When you're alone, your awareness of time and boundaries grows fuzzy. "All distances, all measures," wrote Rainer Maria Rilke, "change for the person who becomes solitary." These sensations have been described by the ascetics of early Christianity, by Buddhist monks, by transcendentalists and shamans, by Russian *startsy* and Japanese *hijiri,* by solo adventurers, by Native Americans and Inuits reporting on vision quests.

"I become a transparent eyeball," wrote Ralph Waldo Emerson in "Nature." "I am nothing; I see all." Lord Byron called it "the feeling infinite"; Jack Kerouac, in *Desolation Angels,* "the one mind of infinity." The French Catholic priest Charles de Foucauld, who spent fifteen years living in the Sahara Desert, said that in solitude "one empties completely the small house of one's soul." Merton wrote that "the true solitary does not seek himself, but loses himself."

This loss of self was precisely what Knight experienced in the forest. In public, one always wears a social mask, a presentation to the world. Even when you're alone and look in a mirror, you're acting, which is one reason Knight never kept a mirror in his camp. He let go of all artifice; he became no one and everyone.

The past, the land of wistfulness, and the future, the place of yearning, seemed to evaporate. Knight simply existed, for the most part, in the perpetual now. He does not care if people fail to understand what he did in the woods. He didn't do it for us to understand. He wasn't trying to prove a point. There was no point. "You're just there," Knight said. "You *are*."

Tenzin Palmo, who was born Diane Perry, near London, was only the second Western woman to become a Tibetan Buddhist nun. Long retreats are still commended in Buddhism, and the current Dalai Lama wrote that a life of seclusion is "the highest form of spiritual practice." Palmo felt immensely drawn to solitude, and in 1976, when she was thirty-three years old, she moved into a remote cave in the Himalayas of northern India. She ate one meal a day—supplies were occasionally delivered to her—and lived through intense high-alpine winters, spending most of her time meditating. A seven-day blizzard once blocked her cave entrance, threatening asphyxiation.

Palmo remained in the cave for twelve years. She never once lay down; she slept, sitting up, inside a small wooden meditation box. Her solitude, she said, was "the easiest thing in the world." Not for a moment did she want to be anywhere else. She overcame all fear of death, she insisted, and felt liberated. "The more you realize, the more you realize there is nothing to realize," she said. "The idea that there's somewhere we have got to get to, and something we have to attain, is our basic delusion."

The British naturalist Richard Jefferies spent much of his short life—he died of tuberculosis in 1887, at age thirty-eight—walking alone in the woods of England. Some of his ideas seemed to parallel Knight's. Jefferies wrote, in his autobiography *The Story of My Heart,* that the type of life celebrated by society, one of hard work and unceasing chores and constant routine, does nothing but "build a wall about the mind." Our whole lives, Jefferies said, are wasted traveling in endless small circles; we are all "chained like a horse to an iron pin in the ground." The richest person, Jefferies believed, is the one who works least. "Idleness," he wrote, "is a great good."

For Jefferies, like Knight, the desire to be alone was an irresistible tug. "My mind required to live its own life apart from other things," wrote Jefferies. In solitude, he said, he could ponder ideas that allowed him to "go higher than a god, deeper than prayer"; there was nothing greater than to stand alone, "bare-headed before the sun, in the presence of the earth and air, in the presence of the immense forces of the universe."

But isolation has a razor's edge. For others, for those who do not choose to be alone—for prisoners and hostages—a loss of one's socially created identity can be terrifying, a plunge into madness. Psychologists call it "ontological insecurity," losing your grip on who you are. Edward Abbey, in *Desert Solitaire,* a chronicle of two six-month stints as a ranger in Utah's Arches National Monument, said that being solitary for a long time and fully attuned to the natural world "means risking everything human." Those who fear this will feel only loneliness, the pain of social isolation, rather than experiencing solitude, which can be by turns exhilarating and turbulent.

"I was never lonely," said Knight. He was attuned to the completeness of his own presence rather than to the absence of others. Conscious thought was sometimes replaced with a soothing internal humming. "Once you taste solitude, you don't grasp the idea of being alone," he said. "If you like solitude, you're never alone. Does that make sense? Or is that one of those koan thingies I'm doing again?"

In an attempt to gain some empirical understanding of solitude, a cognitive neuroscientist at New York University placed more than twenty Buddhist monks and nuns inside magnetic resonance imaging machines, tracking blood flow to their brains while they meditated. Other neuroscientists conducted similar studies. The results remain preliminary, but it appears that when the human brain experiences a self-consciously chosen silence, as opposed to sleep, the brain does not slow down. It remains as active as ever. What changes is *where* the brain is functioning.

Language and hearing are seated in the cerebral cortex, the folded gray matter that covers the first couple of millimeters of the outer brain like wrapping paper. When one experiences silence, absent even reading, the cerebral cortex typically rests. Meanwhile, deeper and more ancient brain structures seem to be activated—the subcortical zones. People who live busy, noisy lives are rarely granted access to these areas. Silence, it appears, is not the opposite of sound. It is another world altogether, literally offering a deeper level of thought, a journey to the bedrock of the self.

While sitting slump-shouldered on his stool in the visiting booth of the jail, speaking of his inner voyages, Knight seemed to be in an introspective mood. I wondered, despite his aversion to dispensing wisdom, if he'd be willing to share more of what he learned while alone. People have been approaching hermits with this request for thousands of years, eager to consult with someone whose life has been so radically different. James Joyce wrote in *A Portrait of the Artist as a Young Man* that a solitary person is able to tap into "the wild heart of life."

Responses from hermits have often been elusive. Tenzin Palmo, pressed for her conclusions about living silently in a cave for a dozen years, said only, "Well, it wasn't boring." Ralph Waldo Emerson wrote, "He that thinks most, will say least." The *Tao Te Ching* says, "Those who know do not tell; those who tell do not know." The great computer Deep Thought, in Douglas Adams's *Hitchhiker's Guide to the Galaxy,* worked on the problem for seven and a half million years, then revealed that the answer to life, the universe, and everything was the number forty-two.

Now it felt like my turn to ask. Was there some grand insight, I questioned Knight, revealed to him in the wild? I was serious about the request. Profound truths, or at least those that make sense of the seeming randomness of life, have always eluded me. What Knight had done was like what Thoreau had—it may, in fact, be the men's similarities that is the source of Knight's contempt. Thoreau wrote in *Walden* that he had reduced existence to its basic elements so that he could "live deep and suck out all the marrow of life."

Maybe, I thought, Knight would talk about the marrow.

He sat quietly, whether thinking or fuming or both, it was

hard to tell. But he eventually arrived at a reply. It felt like some great mystic was about to reveal the Meaning of Life.

"Get enough sleep," he said.

He set his jaw in a way that conveyed he wouldn't be saying any more. This was what he'd learned. I accepted it as truth.

23

Conscious of time's flow or not, Knight was still subject to its laws. He grew older. His survival skills peaked, his efficiency was honed, but like an athlete in decline, his body could not keep pace. For a while he was able to haul two propane tanks on his back. Then he could carry only one.

His eyesight was a constant concern. He'd had poor vision since his youth and was obsessive about protecting his eyeglasses. "I knew if I broke my glasses that would be it," he said, "and that carefulness extended to my whole body." Then, without humor—his preferred way of framing a quip—he added, "No cartwheels over boulders for me."

Even so, the world beyond an arm's length gradually lost focus. His glasses eventually failed him, and everything in the woods became more or less a blur. Each time he saw a pair of glasses during a break-in, he tried them on, but he never found a better prescription. He'd always used his ears more than his eyes, so by the time he couldn't see well, it didn't matter much. He was in his home territory. "Do you need glasses to move about your home? No. I didn't, either."

Most hermits across history, secular ones especially, did not grow old in seclusion. They waited until they were already fairly old, with a stockpile of experience and wisdom, to leave the world. Knight vanished at twenty and never again received a word of guidance or instruction. He turned to no elder for advice. He was king and janitor of his tiny realm, and the rest of the world, he believed, had nothing to teach him, no wonder to offer. His decisions were purely his own.

He sacrificed college, a career, a wife, children, friends, vacations, cars, sex, movies, phones, and computers. He had never in his life sent an e-mail or even seen the internet. His milestones were less significant. Knight switched, at some point, from drinking tea to coffee. Classical music, he eventually realized, soothed him more than rock did. His pet mushroom grew. The handheld game players he stole got smaller and better. He knew, even with blurry vision, when each bald eagle pair nesting in his forest had hatchlings. He began to drink more alcohol.

He fell a couple of times, hard, though never broke a bone. Once he slipped on some ice and banged his left arm so badly he couldn't pick up a cup for a month, but that was the worst injury he sustained. As he aged, the usual bruises on his hands and wrists from living outdoors seemed to linger; they didn't heal the way they used to. His teeth constantly hurt.

Questions crept into his mind. He wondered if all the sugar he was eating was making him diabetic. He thought about cancer, or the possibility of a heart attack, yet he did not consider seeing a doctor. He accepted his mortality as is.

His thieving raids became considerably more challenging,

as cabin owners upgraded locks and installed security systems that were far more complex than any he'd dealt with during his brief time in the workplace. Surveillance cameras became both difficult to incapacitate and widely used.

And despite his fanatical caution on his thieving raids, during which the primary rule was never to break into an occupied cabin, the law of averages began to catch up with him. He finally experienced what he called "an anomaly." Or maybe he got a touch sloppy or overconfident, after so many hundreds of successes.

One midweek summer evening in 2012, Kyle McDougle, whose family has owned property on North Pond for generations, decided to stay alone at the family's cabin. McDougle was twenty at the time, and had heard hermit stories all his life. His grandfather especially liked telling them. McDougle was working for a fiber-optics firm, driving around in a big company truck that couldn't fit on narrow roads, so he left the rig some distance away. It was probably the only time in his life, McDougle says, that he didn't park a vehicle in the cabin's driveway. He crawled into a sleeping bag in the cabin's upstairs loft.

"I wake up and I hear someone on the stairs and I see a flashlight," recalled McDougle. He shouted a greeting and got no response, and knew right away it wasn't a family member showing up in the middle of the night. "I didn't have a flashlight, or a knife, or a gun, and I'm trapped upstairs, so my immediate thought was to scare him, so I yelled, 'Get the hell out of here!' plus a whole bunch of swearwords, shouting at the top of my lungs." With this, the intruder immediately retreated or maybe tumbled down the stairs—"It was *bang, bang, bang, bang, bang,*" said McDougle—and fled out of the cabin.

McDougle never saw the trespasser, but he noted that the screen was popped out of one of the cabin's windows and propped against a wall. "I was obviously very freaked out. I called the police, but there wasn't a heck of a lot they could do."

Knight felt terrible about the incident. "I hate to think that I scared someone like that," he said. "That really bothers me."

As Knight aged, the population of North Pond gradually increased, a few more homes built or expanded each year, families growing, more people in the forest. Knight was alert for unusual sounds. He often heard hikers, but not too near his camp, and on those rare occasions when he sensed a person while he was moving through the trees, he had plenty of time to dash away and quietly hide.

Except once. It was during the day, sometime in the 1990s, before he began walking almost exclusively at night and never on trails. He was on a lightly traveled path, and came around a bend, and with no advance warning, there was someone else. Knight can't say what the hiker looked like—he made no eye contact. He tried to put on a nonchalant face, but he felt panicky. Neither man stopped. Knight said, "Hi," and the man said, "Hi," and they continued on their separate ways.

This was his only encounter for more than twenty years. Then, during a cold winter day, while Knight was ensconced in his camp, he heard a group of people in the forest, postholing through the snow. The steps grew louder and nearer, tree branches snapping like firecrackers, Knight's distress rising, until he made the decision to step out of his camp and assess the situation. He didn't want to be seen, but he couldn't risk anyone stumbling upon his home.

He walked a dozen quiet steps and there they were, breathing heavily in the crisp air. Three men, three generations of the same family—son, father, and grandfather—tromping happily through the woods after a day of ice fishing. Knight ducked down, he said, but it was too late. He'd been spotted. According to Knight, one of the men shouted, "Hey!"

Knight stood. He had on a black ski cap and a blue jacket over a hooded sweatshirt and was clean-shaven. The father, Roger Bellavance, held up his hands, one clutching a pair of binoculars, demonstrating that he had no gun. Knight's hands had been in his pockets, but he pulled them out. He showed that he had no weapon, either. "I tried to convey the idea that I was harmless, no threat, using only my hands. I did not come close to them." Knight insisted that he did not speak a word— "I communicated nonverbally"—though the Bellavances re-called him a mumbling a few phrases.

The grandfather, Tony Bellavance, sensed immediately that they'd encountered the North Pond hermit. He knew the legend; he realized that cabins had been robbed. But in the presence of the hermit himself, Bellavance, who was convinced that the hermit was a military veteran, was struck with a very strong idea of what needed to be done.

"He said we had to leave him alone," recalled the father. "He said that he's not hurting anyone. He's up here for a reason, he said, and he doesn't want to deal with people. My father's a little Frenchman with a big heart, and he just thought this guy needed to be on his own, unbothered." The son and father did not want to go against the grandfather's wishes, so they did what he asked.

The three men all promised out loud that they would let the hermit be. "We made an oath," said the grandfather. "We swore we would never say anything."

The hermit nodded. Then, his arms still held out, palms open, as if ready to catch a beach ball, he leaned forward at the waist and bowed before the three men. "I don't know why I bowed," said Knight. "To convey the idea of thanks, I think." The entire encounter lasted no more than a couple of minutes.

The ice fishermen kept their promise, though Roger, the father, did tell his wife, who was unsure whether he was speaking the truth. No one took a photo or video. Roger said that later he had to fight the urge, several times, to return to the woods and try to talk to the hermit. But he respected Knight's privacy. The men said nothing until after Knight was arrested; then Roger, thinking he might be able to help law enforcement find the campsite, told Trooper Vance the story. She didn't believe it.

Knight said that he hadn't mentioned this incident with the ice fishermen to anyone because he felt that their pact remained in place. The agreement, the way he understood it, was that no one would ever say anything. But I'd just informed Knight, during a visit in the county jail, our seventh one in eight weeks, that the Bellavances had, in fact, spoken to others about it. Knight now felt that the pact was broken.

"What about other pacts?" I asked. "Did more people find you?"

"No, there were no other encounters," Knight swore. People had been looking for him for years. If there'd been any hint that anyone had found his site, word would have spread in a flash.

"Will you make a pact with me that you're not covering up any others?"

"Yes."

The ice-fishermen encounter seemed like just the sort of event for which Knight had established his emergency cache. He could have abandoned his camp well before the men saw him and moved somewhere else. Or he could have decamped immediately after.

He said he seriously thought about evacuating, but there was a lot of snow. "To move, I'd have to leave footprints. I had little food. I took a chance they were good people." Also, Knight admitted, the notion of starting over seemed exhausting. Had he been younger, he almost certainly would've moved. This was when he understood, he said, that "the circle was closing in."

Just two months after seeing the ice fishermen, as the snow was receding and the chickadees had started to sing, with his food supplies nearing zero, Knight departed on a midnight thieving raid. He pried open a rear door of the Pine Tree dining hall. He filled his backpack and stepped out, and was suddenly blinded by a light while someone yelled at him to get on the ground.

24

The ice fishermen did not believe that Knight deserved to be jailed. "If I had a million dollars," said the grandfather, Tony Bellavance, "I'd buy a hundred acres, two hundred acres, and I'd put him right in the middle, and put posted signs around, and let him live like he wants." Bellavance, who is in his seventies, owns a home in the area, but he was never a victim of Knight's crimes.

Harvey Chesley, the facilities director of the Pine Tree Camp, which suffered by far the most losses, had similar feelings. "I always thought that if I caught him in the act, I might let him go," said Chesley. "It was frozen lasagna and a can of beans—not earth-shattering. He was a thief of necessity. He has my respect."

Lisa Fitzgerald, the owner of the property where Knight camped, said the discovery that a stranger had lived on her land for decades was "nothing to be upset about." If she'd found him, she said, she might not have called the police, or even evicted him.

Locals who recognized Knight's story as truth tended to

have gentle reactions. They said that Knight's feat stirred the imagination. At the end of a serene weekend on North Pond, you can't help but envision quitting your job and remaining there for life. Everyone dreams of dropping out of the world once in a while. Then you get in the car and drive back home.

Knight stayed. Yes, he repeatedly broke the law to sustain his escape, but he was never violent. He did not carry a weapon. He didn't even want to see anybody. He was a compulsive introvert, not a hardened criminal. He followed a very strange calling and held true to himself more fully than most of us will ever dare to. He clearly had no desire to be a part of our world.

A couple of residents pledged to provide Knight with land to live on. Let's hold a fund-raiser, others suggested, and give him enough cash to purchase several years' worth of groceries, so he won't need to steal. He should immediately be released from jail and allowed back into the woods. He never harmed anyone.

Physically, that is. Other locals were enraged by Knight's actions. The actual items he stole might be minor, but he also took people's peace of mind. Their sense of security. Some said they were afraid to sleep in their own cabins, afraid for decades.

"I felt violated, over and over and over again," said Debbie Baker, who has owned a place on North Pond with her husband for more than twenty years. "I lost count how many times he broke in." Her two sons, when they were young, were terrified of the hermit. They had nightmares about him. The family installed security lights and dead bolts and even had a police officer spend much of the night, but nothing worked. "I hate what this man did to us," Baker said.

Martha Patterson, whose cabin was a frequent target, said that Knight stole some of the silverware she'd inherited from her mother, and a couple of cherished hand-sewn quilts, but the real damage went deeper. All Patterson wanted from her cabin was a place to escape the pressures of daily life, and Knight denied her that. "I couldn't leave my windows open, I couldn't even go and sit by the beach without worrying," she said. "He stole every bit of my piece of heaven."

"If someone needed food," said Mary Hinkley, a victim of dozens of break-ins, "I would give them food. Just ask. But we were invaded, completely invaded. I always feared he'd come in the night, when my grandchildren were there. I despise this person. I'm ashamed I feel this way, but I do. I can't think of anything in my life I've been so bitter about."

If Knight really wanted to live in the woods, many said, he should've done so on public lands, hunting and fishing for food. And how was anyone supposed to know he wasn't armed and dangerous? Even a single break-in can be punishable by a ten-year prison sentence. Knight was nothing but a lazy man and a thief times a thousand. He should be locked up in the state penitentiary, perhaps for life.

The person who was going to decide what punishment, if any, to seek against Knight was Maeghan Maloney, the district attorney. Maloney grew up in Maine, in a blue-collar family, living in subsidized housing. She was the valedictorian of her high school class and won a scholarship to Harvard Law. She'd heard public opinion on Knight—free him now, incarcerate him forever—and she, too, was conflicted. "In a lot of ways," said Maloney, "the law is not set up for an outlier case like this."

Knight himself was not seeking leniency. "There's no justification for my stealing," he said. "And I don't want people trying to justify my bad behavior in an attempt not to sully what they admire in me. Take the whole package, good and bad. Judge me on that. Don't cherry-pick. Don't make excuses for me."

"*Everyone* makes excuses," said Terry Hughes, who witnessed Knight's confession in the Pine Tree dining room. "Criminals will deny, deny, deny. That's what you deal with when you deal with criminals. That's the world we live in. I'm used to that world."

Hughes said that he had never encountered a person as guilelessly straightforward about his crimes as Knight. He just owned up to everything, Hughes pointed out. Knight had no problem admitting to a thousand burglaries. He understood that it was wrong, he was embarrassed and remorseful, but there was total acknowledgment. "Everything in my gut wanted to hate this guy," said Hughes. "I'm a typical stubborn jarhead. He stole food from a camp for disabled people. But I can't hate him. You could work in law enforcement a hundred years and never come across anyone like this."

"It's a very strange case, for sure," said Knight's pro bono defender, Walter McKee, who is renowned in Maine for his work ethic and his expertise. McKee arrives at his office each day at three-fifteen a.m. He is also a classical violinist, a mountaineer, a private airplane pilot, a father, and a husband.

"Mr. McKee does not sleep," reports his firm's website. He consented to waive Knight's right to a speedy trial in order to determine how best to proceed.

The modern hermit community—it exists—also debated Knight's merits. On the Hermitary website is an area called Hermit's Slate, which is described as "a forum for hermits, solitaries, anchorites, recluses, introverts." Before you're allowed to post there, the administrator of the Hermitary site, who uses the pen name Meng-hu, must decide whether you are a legitimate hermit. There are currently more than a thousand members; perhaps not surprisingly, there are seldom more than two or three online at once.

The general consensus among Hermitary denizens seems to be that Knight should not be considered a hermit. He was more of an insult to hermits. Meng-hu wrote a blog post about hermits like Knight. "The idea of a hermit who steals for a living confirms the worst stereotype of the 'eremite as parasite,'" noted Meng-hu. "No historical hermit, especially those motivated by a spiritual sense but also wilderness hermits, has ever had the slightest motive to encroach upon anybody's belongings—be that body, mind, time, space, or goods." Stealing, added Meng-hu, is universally condemned by other hermits because it shows that one is undisciplined, lacking in empathy, and a menace to society, which are all contradictory to hermit ideals.

Knight, official hermit or not, was unable to afford bail, so he remained in the Kennebec County jail. Within days of being locked up, he caught a debilitating head cold, but after that his immune system kicked in, and he managed to avoid further illness. He received a new pair of glasses, his first in thirty years, with oval lenses and silver wire frames.

He lost weight, and became as gaunt as after a grim winter in the woods. Now that food was freely given to him, he joked, he couldn't eat; but the truth was that jail made him too nervous to have an appetite. He was a model inmate, says Chief Deputy Sheriff Ryan Reardon. His beard—his timepiece and his disguise—grew wildly, and ever more itchy, but he refused to shave.

Knight had figured that both his parents had died while he was in the woods, but soon after his capture, Diane Vance, who'd run a background check, told him that his mother, Joyce Knight, was still alive. She was in her eighties. Chris begged Vance not to contact her, or anyone else in his family, and she agreed. He wished to remain a secret, even in jail.

Six days after his arrest, Knight was informed by Vance that the story had leaked. His mother would soon learn about him through the media. Knight gave Vance permission to notify his mom that he'd been found.

She telephoned Mrs. Knight. "I didn't beat around the bush," said Vance. "I just broke the news to her. I think she was in shock, because it's quite possible she thought he was dead. Then I think she ended up being mad because he was in jail, and had been committing crimes. I remember her saying, 'At my age, it's a lot to take in.'"

Knight accepted a single jail visit from his brothers Joel and Timothy. It was Joel who had co-signed the loan on the Brat that Chris had abandoned. According to Kerry Vigue, the family friend, Joel paid off the full amount owed and never pressed charges. "Joel thought that was not a brotherly thing to do," Vigue noted.

Chris did not allow his mother to come. He said that a visit with his mother would cause her shame and grief. "Look at me: I'm in my prison clothes. I couldn't let her see me like this. I'm a thief, I'm in jail, guilty of so many crimes. This is not something my mom raised me to be. This is no place for her."

It was for the same reason, Knight said, that he never phoned home the whole time he was in the woods. "Because who I was"—a hermit, a thief—"would offend my family's belief system. It would embarrass them. I couldn't tell them." Instead, he allowed his family to wonder endlessly, to ache; a confounding choice.

He decided that he would see his mother only once he was released from jail, so they could speak "properly, face-to-face." But after six months of imprisonment, he had no idea when that might be. His skin had broken out in hives, and his hands sometimes trembled. Just finding out how many more seasons he'd be spending locked up might have reduced some of his stress, but he understood the delay. "I don't fit into any categories," he said. "Apparently, they don't get a lot of hermits these days." So he sank back into himself, clutching the threads of his sanity, waiting to learn of his fate.

25

A side door to the jail swings open and three sheriff's deputies emerge, armed and wearing bulletproof vests, along with a prisoner, hands cuffed in front, his beard like Spanish moss. One deputy stations himself ahead of Knight, the other two grip each elbow, and they march him across Court Street toward the Kennebec County Courthouse, with its sentry of granite columns. Red and yellow leaves scatter in the fall breeze, and television cameras are shoved into Knight's face, but he manages to remain impassive, his gaze directed at some unseen spot in front of him.

The upstairs courtroom is all dark wood and maroon carpeting, with a giant brick fireplace in one corner, the walls a haunted-house display of oil paintings of old judges staring sternly from gilded frames. A memorial service was held here to commemorate Abraham Lincoln after his assassination in 1865.

Wooden pews in the back creak with spectators, and the press photography and television section is full, everyone awaiting Knight's arrival. Boxes of files are carried about.

McKee, Knight's attorney, wears a dark suit; Maloney, the DA, a fire-engine-red jacket. Knight's brother Joel—same thin lips, same sharp nose—sits with his son and daughter, both of whom look to be in their twenties. This is the first time they will see their uncle. The son's leg bounces, and I overhear Joel saying, "Nerves. Perfectly normal."

Knight is brought in, stationed behind the defense table, and uncuffed. The room quiets. A court officer says, "All rise," and Justice Nancy Mills appears like a magic trick through a red curtain hanging over a doorway. She smooths her black robe and sits down, then sets a pair of reading glasses low on her nose and begins. For those not charting moons or seasons or chin hair, it's Monday, October 28, 2013, nearly seven months after Knight's arrest.

A solution has been found. Knight will plead guilty to thirteen counts of burglary and theft—the vast majority of his raids could not be prosecuted because of a six-year statute of limitations and many were never reported at all—and instead of going to prison, he will be admitted into the Co-Occurring Disorders and Veterans Court.

This is a program that substitutes counseling and judicial monitoring for incarceration, designed for defendants facing criminal charges who are also affected by substance abuse and mental illness—the co-occurring disorders. In Knight's case, his afflictions are alcoholism and either Asperger's syndrome, depression, or schizoid personality disorder. These labels may not be precisely accurate, but even the DA agrees that a long prison sentence for Knight would be cruel, and admitting him to the program is a way to legally resolve the case.

Knight stands, clasps his hands behind his back, and Maloney reads the charges. If it weren't for the gravity of the proceedings, they might sound humorous.

"On or about July 14, 2008," Maloney intones, "Mr. Edmund Ashley reported items stolen from his camp in Rome, Maine. The items stolen were batteries, food, and soda, with an approximate value of eighteen dollars."

Justice Mills asks for Knight's plea.

"Guilty," he says, scarcely audible.

"A seasonal resident's kitchen window had been forced open," Maloney continues, "and food items, along with a pair of men's size thirty-eight jeans and a leather belt, had been stolen, with a value of approximately forty dollars."

"Guilty."

On it goes, eleven more times. "Are you pleading guilty because you are guilty and for no other reason?" asks Justice Mills when it's done.

"Yes."

"Do you understand what we're doing?"

"Yes."

"I am satisfied that Mr. Knight's pleas are voluntary," says Mills. Then she reviews the conditions of his sentence. Knight will serve a total of seven months in jail—he has another week to go—and, once released, must seek psychological counseling. He needs to call his case manager every day. He has to appear in court every Monday at eleven a.m. so Mills can review his progress. These rules will be in effect for at least one year, and if he breaks any of them, he could be subject to as much as a seven-year term in the state prison.

He is also fined a total of about $2,000, to be distributed to his victims. He will live at home, with his mother, and must find a job or go to school, and he must perform community service. He may not contact any of his victims or leave the state of Maine, and he is prohibited from using or possessing alcohol. He will be subject to random drug and alcohol testing.

"Obviously," Mills adds, "you can't get involved in any further criminal trouble of any kind—do you understand that, Mr. Knight?"

"Yes."

"Any questions or anything else you would like to say, Mr. Knight?"

"No," he says, and the hearing is over.

A few hours later, I visit Knight in jail for the final time. It's our ninth one-hour visit over the course of two months, encompassing four trips to Maine. There are telephones in jail, but he has steadfastly refused to make a call, though we speak through receivers during our visits. He hasn't placed a phone call in thirty years, and even before he went into the woods, he didn't like phones.

"People earnestly say to me here, 'Mr. Knight, we have cell phones now, and you're going to really enjoy them.' That's their enticement for me to rejoin society. 'You're going to love it,' they say. I have no desire. And what about a text message? Isn't that just using a telephone as a telegraph? We're going backwards." When he hears how songs are now shared and downloaded, Knight is equally unimpressed. "You're using your computers, your thousand-dollar machines, to listen to the radio? Society is taking a rather strange turn." He says he'll stick with vinyl records.

With his release imminent, Knight seems more unsettled than ever. He scratches furiously at his knees. Jail, he's realized, might not be all bad. There's routine and order in jail, and he's able to click into a survival mode that is not too dissimilar, in terms of steeliness of mental state, to the one he'd perfected during winters in the woods. "I'm surrounded in here by less than desirable people," he says, "but at least I wasn't thrown into the waters of society and expected to swim."

Now he is being tossed into public life, and he's frightened. It's not the big things, like getting a job or relearning to drive, that worry him but the little ones, like eye contact and gestures and emotions, all of which can be badly misinterpreted. "I'm extremely emotionally thin-skinned. I need therapy. I realize that."

He feels like the stakes are high for him—he's fearful that he is going to make a mistake that will send him to prison. The punishment looms over him like a guillotine. "I have no preparation for re-entry into society. I don't know your world. Only my world, and memories of the world before I went to the woods. What is life today? What is proper? There are blank spots in my skill set. I have to figure out how to live."

He refers to what's happening to him, literally and metaphorically, as his "double winter." He was arrested as one winter was ending and will be released as the next is beginning. "It's going to be a year without summer. Like when Krakatoa blew."

He's been invited into the family home, to the sixty-acre

plot in the town of Albion, back to his boyhood bedroom. "They don't approve of what I did, but I am still part of the family. I am grateful." He will move in with his mother and his sister, with his brother Daniel close by. Even after decades, his home looms large in his memory. He saw a picture of the house in a newspaper story and noticed right away that it had been painted a slightly different color.

He is unimpressed with what he's learned in jail of the society he is about to enter, and is certain he is not going to fit in. Everything moves at light speed, without rest. "It's too loud. Too colorful. The lack of aesthetics. The crudeness. The inanities. The trivia. The inappropriate choices of aspirations and goals."

He admits that he's really not in a position to judge. He says that when he is released, he is going to avoid even the intimation of wrongdoing; he will hew to the law and keep clean. "I don't want people questioning my questionable judgment."

His job prospects, he knows, are dim. "Money, huh? I've got to reacquire the taste for money. I intend to get a job. But my résumé is rather thin." He has low expectations of employment, low and slow. Washing dishes, stocking shelves.

He was actually offered a sort of internship while in jail. The owner of a local organic farm contacted the DA's office and said she had an idea to introduce Knight to her style of growing crops. The farm is plowed by horse and oxen, and has a roadside stand that sells homemade pies, jams, and sundried-tomato pesto. There are sleigh rides for kids in winter. The owner spoke of how the farm healed her family, and she thought it could do the same for Knight. She was permitted to present the offer to Knight in person at the jail.

Knight tried his hardest, he says, to remain polite and cooperative during the meeting. "I talked farming. I know about farming. I talked about the whole hippie-experience thing, the back-to-the-land movement, worshipping nature. I think I gave her the wrong idea that I wanted to work in the fields."

Neighbors of the farm, according to Knight, were nervous about the notion of him being there, and the owner rescinded the offer. Knight was pleased that the crop-picking idea collapsed. "Me bent over in the hot fields after all those years in the shade of the woods was not going to happen."

I tell Knight that I can research employment opportunities for him, quiet jobs like security guard or librarian, and he shakes his head vigorously no. "Please leave me alone," he says. The best thing I can do is not help him. Help is a kind of relationship. Next thing you know I'll be asking to be his friend, and he doesn't want to be my friend. "I'm not going to miss you at all," he adds.

He is a connoisseur of the arc of the seasons and the scent of the wind, but he can't really see anyone else. I've told him a little about my family and my pastimes, and he didn't even bother to feign much interest. He doesn't know what to do with the information, what questions to ask. He knows people only peripherally, by the food in their pantry and the decorations on their walls. His only real relationship was between him and the forest.

Knight thinks of himself both as a common criminal and as a Nietzschean *Übermensch*—a superman, subject to no one else's rules, a master of self-discipline capable of transcending the vapidity of life. He has told me his story and asked for nothing in return, but he admits that he wonders which version of him I will portray. "I'm worried about having my identity applied by someone else," he says. "I don't particularly trust you. I don't distrust you, either. I'm taking measure of the man. There are certain threadbare spots in your measure. You have the ability to do harm or good. Do what you think is right."

He really only had a single curiosity about me: What books were on my shelves? He asks me to take a video of them and send it to him. He says he'll find a way to get the technology to work. Make the video, he says, but mail no more books or letters, and certainly do not pay a visit to his home. "Once I get out of here, you're off my dance card. I can't afford the indulgence that is you; I deny you my magnificent presence. Did you get my dance-card reference, or do I have to update my references? Did you read *Little Women*?"

He especially detests my aggressiveness, my coming to speak with him so many times. "You get a bee in your bonnet, and there's no stopping you." He says that he regrets writing back to me. Then he backpedals. He fears, he adds, that he is being too hostile. He did get something out of the visits: "Some stress release." But he has grown weary of talking about himself.

Mostly what he wants me to do is just slow down and let time pass. "Don't be a pest," he says. "I'll speak to you when the lilacs bloom. And maybe not even then." I ask him if by lilacs blooming he means next year, and he says, "Yes, in spring. I don't use years yet."

Knight is no longer able to disappear into the wild, not without risking seven years in prison, so he wishes to melt into the world. A guard comes to escort him away, and I thank him for speaking with me, for sharing his ideas. For the lyricism of his language. I tell him I like the way his mind works. "Good-bye, Chris," I say. "Good luck."

There is time for Knight to express a last thought. He does not. There's no wave, no nod. He stands up, turns his back on me, and walks out of the visiting booth and down a corridor of the jail.

26

Chris's oldest brother, Daniel, provides him with a job. Daniel runs a scrap-metal-recycling business, and he begins hauling old automobile and tractor engines to Chris, who takes them apart in a shed on his family's property. He is not getting paid; it's in exchange for room and board. But he works alone, fulfilling his employment requirement without social interaction.

Each Monday, a family member drives him to Augusta for his meeting at the courthouse. He never misses one, and he's never late. He follows the rules of his punishment to the letter. "He is doing a remarkable job," says Maeghan Maloney. "He has been working hard to understand what it takes to become part of society again. He hasn't had a single setback. I often see him on Mondays and say hi. We always talk a bit. He seems to be content." He registers to vote, as an independent.

Phil Dow, the president of the Albion Historical Society, has known the Knight family for fifty years. Joyce Knight calls him one day and asks if there's any work Chris might do, to accomplish his community service. "I told her I'd love to have him," says Dow.

About once a week, Dow drives to Knight's home and brings him to the train station. The village of Albion, enthuses Dow, has one of the few remaining narrow-gauge railroad stations in the world. The tracks are two feet apart, less than half the standard dimension—easier and cheaper to lay across difficult terrain. Passengers and freight were transported on this line through central Maine from the late 1800s until June 15, 1933, when a train going around a curve broke the outside rail and tumbled down a bank of the Sheepscot River. The Albion Historical Society is restoring the cedar-sided two-story station.

Knight is volunteering as a painter. "He doesn't talk much," says Dow. "Though I don't really let him because I'm such a ratchet jaw. But he seems happy."

While Knight was still in jail, a woman named Alice Macdonald, who went to high school with him, sent him a letter. She was a couple of years older, she wrote, but she remembered Knight and hoped to conduct Bible-study lessons with him. Knight did not want the lessons, but something about Macdonald interested him. She wasn't prying to get at his story and seemed to have no ulterior motives. She knew him from before the woods. She was female. They met several times at the jail, his only other regular visitor, and Knight continues to see her.

"So you have a girlfriend," I'd teased, feather gentle, during our final jailhouse meeting.

"No, I'm not engaging in a romance, if that nasty little thought crossed your mind," Knight replied, knocked over by my feather. The visits with Macdonald were also non-contact, the window between them. He did say he preferred speaking with a woman. "She's a nice lady. She provides me comfort. She got emotional one day and said, 'I wish I could hug you.' I found the idea of her touching me to be an alien idea."

Knight's double winter progresses, and I fulfill his assignment by filming all the books in my house, sixteen minutes of unviral video. I mail the disc to him but hear nothing back. I don't even know if it reaches him. Every time I hike in the forest, and others times too, I wonder how he's doing. "The state can run him through programs," said Terry Hughes, "and he may do fine, but then again, on some Monday or Tuesday morning, he could walk out the door and go back to the woods." I keep expecting to hear that he's gone, but the news never comes.

I telephone Daniel Knight to inquire about Chris. Daniel answers, and I introduce myself and he says, "No thanks," and hangs up. His brother Jonathan, who lives in Fairbanks, Alaska, hangs up without a word. Timothy never answers.

Joel Knight runs an auto-repair shop in the tourist town of Belfast, on the Maine coast. I take a trip to Maine in which I do not contact Chris but drive over to Joel's shop and walk in. There's a flurry of activity in the four-bay garage, but Joel is easy to spot, in a black T-shirt, dipping in and out of the rear of an SUV, holding a drill, then a wrench, moving fluidly about the small space inside the vehicle. Natural physical grace seems to run in the Knight family.

"He's a genius with my Prius," says the co-owner of Left Bank Books, the town's independent bookstore. The co-owner says that of course everyone in town knows about Joel's brother. "I could never ask him about Chris," she adds. "I don't know Joel that well." She does, however, share the town rumor, likely apocryphal, that Chris's mother continued to celebrate his birthday, even with a cake, for many years.

I walk across the garage and introduce myself to Joel, and I see from the look on his face—not mean but firm—that we aren't going to speak much. His hands are dirty, and we don't shake. Joel does confirm that no one in his family ever knew where Chris was, and that as far as he knows, no one ever helped Chris, no one saw him, and anyone who thinks he's lying is mistaken. It is clear from his tone that he doesn't understand Chris's actions, either.

"When did you start to believe that Chris had died?"

"That's personal."

"What was it like when he returned home?"

"That's personal." Joel slips back into the car, conversation over.

I also stop by Chris's girlfriend Alice Macdonald's house. She opens her front door and says, "I can't speak with you," and closes it.

When I call his mother and tell her I'd like to chat about Chris, she says, "I understand," and disconnects me. Phil Dow, of the historical society, says that Joyce Knight told him it's good to have Chris back. She reported that his appetite has returned and he's been devouring the groceries. "She loves to see him eat," says Dow.

One thing does elicit a response. I mail Chris a holiday card, with a photo of my three children, and a couple of weeks later I receive a note, written in familiar shaky print, black ink on a white index card. "Such a display of beauty and happiness is not possible without contentment," he says about the holiday card. He refers to my children, endearingly, as "the cowboys." "Well done," he adds. "Solstice greetings? Acknowledgment? Whatever." There is no name, as usual, but it warms me to hear from him. It seems like getting out of jail has softened him a bit.

That note, thirty-four words long, is all I get. Seven months after we parted in jail, I again return to Maine. On the drive from the airport, I stop by the Fox Hill Lilac Nursery and purchase a large sprig of purple lilacs. It's my olive branch. Then I head to Hillman's Bakery in Fairfield and buy an apple pie, a gift for his mother.

Past lumber mills and antiques shops, bed-and-breakfasts and above-ground swimming pools. A couple of wild turkeys strut along the road's shoulder. There are farm eggs for sale on a folding table at the end of a driveway, but no person there—just a box for the money. Central Maine is still on the honor system.

It takes forty seconds to drive the length of Albion's Main Street—post office, library, gas station, church, general store. At the store, a bulletin board has handwritten signs for diesel engine repair, yoga classes, snow removal, and hunting guides. There are no traffic lights. At both ends of the town are clusters of white or tan wood-sided homes set close to the road. Then it's countryside again: a dairy farm, a place that will butcher your deer, a vest-pocket cemetery with a few tombstones nearly two hundred years old.

The Knight house is mostly hidden behind a wall of hedges and trees. Only the second-floor windows, with bright blue shutters, are visible from the road, two rectangular eyes peering out of the greenery. A black mailbox says, "Joyce W. Knight" on it, beside two newspaper boxes, one for the *Portland Press Herald,* one for the *Morning Sentinel.* A giant red maple dominates the front yard.

I pull my rental car into the short dirt drive, in front of a small garage separate from the house that has a weather vane on top and a metal sign that says in embossed letters, "Sheldon C. Knight." The yard is quiet. There's no sign of another vehicle. No one seems to be home. I sit in the car for a moment, wondering what to do. Something about the house makes me nervous, though it's unremarkable in every way, just a boxy wood-sided place, painted pale yellow, with a couple of asphalt roof tiles in need of replacing. I get out of the car, carrying the lilac sprig and the apple pie, and take a few strides toward the front door when out of the bushes, soundlessly, steps Chris Knight.

27

He's shaved, the wild whiskers now a smooth, rounded chin. He is wearing a brown-and-tan plaid flannel shirt tucked into faded blue jeans, and a brown baseball cap with no insignia. He still has the silver-framed bifocals given to him in jail. On his feet are old leather work boots.

I hold out the lilac branch, drooping with flowers, and Knight looks at it crossly. It's like offering a glass of water to a fish. There are lilacs, I now notice, blooming pink, purple, and white everywhere on the Knight property. I lower the branch and lift my other hand, like a waiter, pie box on my palm. "I brought something for your mother," I say.

Knight's eyes slide over to the box. "No," he says firmly. I retreat to my car, open the driver's-side door, set down the lilacs and the pie, and shut the door.

We stand there, unnaturally far apart. "Can I shake your hand?" I ask. We'd never had the chance; a wall had always separated us.

"I'd rather not," Knight answers, so we don't.

Knight indicates, twisting his head, for me to follow him.

We walk behind the garage with the weather vane on top, out of sight of the road, in the perfumy breeze of a lilac tree, branches grazing our heads. The grass is vivid green after a week of rain. Apple trees bloom with white flowers, the forerunners to fruit. Nearby is the weathered wooden shed, sagging, where Knight does his salvage work.

There are swarms of no-see-ums, flying grains of pepper, and I continually brush them away but don't grab or slap. Even during our jail visits I'd tried to keep my gestures in check around Knight, to preserve his calm. His movements were always so clean and careful. Knight seems not at all disturbed by the insects.

Everyone I'd spoken with in his circle, without exception, had exclaimed how ably he was adjusting. He appears healthy and his skin has nice color. He's still thin—the end of his belt dangles—but not emaciated like he once was. The lack of a beard skews him younger. He's been to a dentist; one tooth has been removed, I see, and the rest are shiny and clean. But one of the first things he says is that the optimistic face he's displayed in public is false, another mask. In truth, he's hurting.

"I'm not doing very well," he admits, gazing over my shoulder in his usual manner. Nobody understands him, he tells me. People constantly take offense at what he says. "They misconstrue me as arrogant. I feel like I'm in high school all over again." He sacrificed everything else in the world for complete autonomy, and now he's nearly fifty years old and not allowed to make simple decisions for himself.

The judge, his counselors, and his therapist, says Knight, speak to him as though he's a child. Every time he admitted he was struggling, they fed him platitudes. Knight rattles them off: "Oh, it'll get better. Look on the bright side. The sun will come up tomorrow." He grew tired of hearing them, so now he keeps quiet. He doesn't blame anyone—"everyone's doing their best," he says in a way that can be construed as arrogant—but following their rules causes him to feel worse. Jail, in some sense, was preferable. Now that he's free, it is clear that he isn't.

He reaches into a front pocket of his jeans and pulls out a watch with a broken strap. His family, he says, doesn't want him speaking with me. If they knew I was here, they'd be upset. The timing of my visit is good, but we don't have long. His mother is coming home soon. And then his brother needs to drive him to Augusta for his drug testing. He shakes his head. He's never in his life used illegal drugs, not so much as a toke of pot, yet this is how he must spend his afternoon.

"I am a square peg," he says. Everybody he encounters, he feels, is smashing at him, pounding on him, trying to jam him into a round hole. Society seems no more welcoming to him than before he left. He fears he may be forced to take psycho-tropic medicines, drugs that will mess with his brain, when he already knows exactly how to fix everything.

All he needs to do is return to his camp. Though, of course, he can't. He must perform the whole dog-and-pony show of his punishment. "Am I crazy?" he asks. He says he received the video of my books, but that lately he's not even interested in reading. He asks again: "Am I crazy?"

Knight looks at me and actually holds eye contact for a few beats, and I can read the sadness. While in jail, he had always felt emotionally closed off. Possibly, it was the cumbersome arrangement of the visiting booth—the glass wall, the staticky phone receivers, the lack of privacy. Now his face has taken on a new dimension, no longer cold and off-putting. He is reaching out; he seems to be asking for help.

Maybe the best way to forge a bond with a true hermit is to leave him alone for a while. In jail he was orating, pontificating. Now we are speaking. Some connection has formed. We aren't friends, but perhaps we are acquaintances. By explaining to me how nobody else understood him, he may have hinted that he feels like I do have some understanding.

I say to him, truthfully, that I don't believe he is crazy.

Then, as if to challenge my conclusion, he suddenly asks me a seemingly random question. "What do you think I'm talking about when I say 'the Lady of the Woods'? I'm speaking allegorically."

"Mother Nature," I guess.

"No," he says. "Death."

Knight's question wasn't random. Death, in fact, is the subject he most wants to talk about. He says that he's seen the Lady of the Woods before, during a very bad winter. His food was finished, his propane used up, and the cold was unrelenting. He was in his bed, in his tent, starving, freezing, dying. The Lady appeared. She was wearing a hooded sweater, a feminine Grim Reaper. She lifted an eyebrow and lowered her hood. She asked if he was going with her or staying. He says he's aware, on an intellectual level, that it was just some fevered, desperate hallucination, but he's still not entirely sure.

He tells me he has a plan. He is going to wait for the first really frigid day, probably in late November, six or so months from now, and he will set out into the forest wearing very little clothing. He will walk as deep into the woods as he can. Then he is going to sit down and allow nature to take care of him. He will freeze himself to death. "I'm going to walk with the Lady of the Woods," he says. He thinks about this all the time. He realizes he's caught in an impossible trap: if he seeks liberty by returning to his camp, he'll be locked up. He craves to "touch, embrace, accept relief." He's done some research; hypothermia, he believes, is a painless way to die. "It's the only thing that will make me free."

He stands stiffly, hands in his jean pockets. "Something's got to give," he says. "Or something's going to break." And this is the line that breaks him. His voice catches and his Stoicism crumbles, and the humanity beneath pushes out, and I glance at his face and see tears sliding down his cheeks.

I can't help it. I cry as well. Two grown men standing beneath a lilac tree on a gorgeous spring day. Knight is able, after all, to interact with another person, and do so in the most open and vulnerable way. And right then, I come the closest I think I ever will to understanding why Knight left. He left because the world is not made to accommodate people like him. He was never happy in his youth—not in high school, not with a job, not being around other people. It made him feel constantly nervous. There was no place for him, and instead of suffering further, he escaped. It wasn't so much a protest as a quest; he was like a refugee from the human race. The forest offered him shelter.

"I did it because the alternative was— I wasn't content," says Knight. "I did find a place where I was content."

I think that most of us feel like something is missing from our lives, and I wondered then if Knight's journey was to seek it. But life isn't about searching endlessly to find what's missing; it's about learning to live with the missing parts. Knight had been away too long, and I sensed that there was no coming back. He had a brilliant mind, but all his thinking had only trapped him alone in the woods.

"Yeah, the brilliant man," says Knight, "the brilliant man went to find contentment, and he did. The brilliant man wishes he weren't so stupid to do illegal things to find contentment."

During nearly every visit in the county jail, Knight had chastised me for a few moments about abandoning my wife and the cowboys, neglecting my fatherly duties to talk with him. I'd found it amusing—he had shirked all responsibility entirely—but in the end, he was right. I saw what happened to Knight and felt only the urge to go home.

For Knight, his camp was the one spot on the planet where he knew he belonged. His existence had been extraordinarily challenging at times, but he'd made it work. So he had remained there as long as he could.

He doesn't want to sit in a shed taking apart engines. He has known something far more profound, and that sense of loss feels unbearable. I understand all this, yet I'm powerless to change anything or relieve his pain. We stand there, our tears streaming. He will return to the trees, his real home, even if it is just to die. "I miss the woods," he says.

Knight fishes out his watch once more. He says he probably won't see me ever again. It was risky to speak even this once, against his family's wishes. There won't be another conversation. After he's gone, he says, I can tell his story any way I want. "You're my Boswell," he declares. He no longer cares what's written about him. "I'll be with the Lady of the Woods, I'll be happy," he tells me. "You can make T-shirts with my image on them if you wish, and have your kids sell them on the corner."

I smile at the idea, suspending my tears. The world is a confusing place, meaningful and meaningless at once. "It was good to see you," he says. He walks me around the garage to my car, and leaves me there. His mother will be coming any minute. "Go," he whispers. "Go." And I do.

28

A mile down the road, I pull over. He just told me he was going to kill himself, that he has a detailed plan for it. Now what am I supposed to do: Keep it a secret? Call the police, his family, a caseworker? Do I have a legal responsibility? A moral one? I drive to my hotel in a panic and phone a couple of therapists for advice.

The legal part is clear: a man who says he's going to kill himself in six months is not making an imminent threat. It doesn't matter if Knight passes time like a tree, his six months not like our six months—I could take him to the police or a hospital and they wouldn't hold him against his will.

Morally, things are murkier. To me, Knight is serious about his threat, no question. Catherine Benoist, a clinical psychologist in private practice near Chicago, agrees: "He meets several criteria that would classify him as being at a very high potential for suicide." His need for autonomy, Benoist adds, only amplifies this likelihood, as suicide can be considered the ultimate expression of independence. Thomas Frazier of the Center for Autism in Cleveland seconds this opinion: "He's at very, very high risk for suicide." Peter Deri, the clinical psychologist in New York, says, "I would worry about him."

I worry all night, and in the morning I decide to return to his home and tell him in person that I'm conflicted. We'll talk it out, I'm thinking, like I'd do with a real friend. I drive the rural roads toward Albion, and just before his house I approach his brother's place, where the garage door is open, and inside, tinkering with an engine, is a man: thin, glasses, jeans, baseball cap. It's Chris. I pull over. The man in the garage looks up.

It's not him. It's Daniel. We see each other. I'm stopped on the side of the road, close enough to talk, so I feel like I have little choice but to get out and say hello. I'm pulling the door handle when I notice, up the street, a man frantically waving at me. This time it is Chris. I drive away from Daniel awkwardly, without speaking, and park in front of the garage with the weather vane.

Chris approaches my car and motions for me to lower the window. I do not. I open the door and step out. He's extremely agitated—he witnessed my brief encounter with Daniel and says I've done "terrible damage." Knight's face, I see, has closed again. The previous day, he had been so willing to reveal himself, and now he's snapped shut. I explain that I was afraid of what he'd told me about the Lady of the Woods. "I was just exploring an idea," he says angrily. He's retreating from his threats, it's clear, to get rid of me.

"Go back to Montana," Knight says. "The cowboys need their father. Leave me alone. Now." He walks inside his house without another word, and for the second time in two days I drive back to my hotel upset.

This time I call real estate agents. It doesn't seem healthy for a middle-aged man to live in his childhood room. A tiny cabin, roof caved in, is $16,500. I wonder if he'd accept such a gift, or if his therapist would agree that it's a good idea. He'd still need money, for repairs and food, and he has not a dollar. All of the donations to his cause went to restitution, and he owes more.

Knight had specifically asked me not to interfere in his life, so I veto buying him the cabin and fly home. I write him a letter: "I absolutely cannot stand the thought that you may choose to take a stroll with the Lady of the Woods." I do not tell his caseworker, or anyone else in Knight's life, about the suicide risk, but every month or so I write again, through spring and summer and into fall. There's no reply.

When November arrives, the time of his threat, I can stand it no longer. I book a flight to Maine, and ten days before I leave, I send him a brief note saying I'm on my way. My wife calls me while I'm changing planes in New York. A postcard has arrived from Knight. "'Urgently important that you leave me alone,'" she reads to me over the phone. "'Show me respect by leaving me alone. Please. If you appear I will call police. Leave me alone. Please.'" I fly back without seeing him.

Winter descends, and I try to keep tabs on Knight. Every North Pond resident I speak with says the past two summers without the hermit have been the most carefree in memory. People have been leaving their cabin doors unlocked, like in the old days. "It's just done," says Jodie Mosher-Towle, editor of the twice-yearly bulletin the *North Pond News*. "It's in the past. Nobody wants to hear about the hermit anymore around here, because it's like yeah, whatever." Maloney, the

DA, e-mails to tell me that Knight continues to arrive in court promptly every Monday and is doing fantastically well. So at least I know he's alive.

At the end of winter, Maloney announces that Knight has completed the Co-Occurring Disorders and Veterans Court and on March 23, 2015, he will officially graduate. It's been nearly two years since his arrest at Pine Tree. "His performance in this court has been flawless," Justice Mills says at his final hearing. "There was never a misstep. He has done everything he has been asked to do." Knight is placed on probation for three years, unable to possess alcohol or drugs and required to continue psychological counseling, but with few other restrictions. "Mr. Knight," says Maloney, "is now a member of our community."

Knight sits in the defendant's chair in court, still thin and clean-shaven, but with something different about him. Though he doesn't speak at graduation, his demeanor seems more docile. There is an unfamiliar slackness to his visage. He is wearing a navy blue V-neck sweater over a white button-down, like a kindergarten teacher.

In one of the first letters he wrote me, Knight described himself, in verse, as "defensive, defiant, aggressive, you bet," then added, concluding the rhyme, "but at least not compliant, at least not yet." From the initial moment I encountered Knight, through to the day he told me he wanted to kill himself, he was full of defiance.

Now, in court, he seems compliant. Fighting against everything, he may have realized, only makes one's life infinitely harder. He has seen the bottomless nonsense of our world and has decided, like most of us, to simply try to tolerate it. He appears to have surrendered. It is rational, yet heartbreaking.

After the hearing, I drive by North Pond again. I park my car beside the road and struggle through the snow-choked woods to his camp. It's my eighth trip here; I've spent the night five times, across every season. Now I sense that the site, as with Knight himself, has been scrubbed of some crucial vitality.

The Maine Department of Environmental Protection had recently sent in a six-person team and an all-terrain vehicle and removed the remaining trash and propane tanks, creating more of a human trail in a few hours than Knight did in decades.

It's now just a spot in the woods. One or two more summers and it'll probably be hard to tell that someone lived here. I sit on a boulder, out of the snow, trying to catch a few blades of sunlight slashing through the branches. Still, I shiver. It feels a little lonely here.

Modern life seems set up so that we can avoid loneliness at all costs, but maybe it's worthwhile to face it occasionally. The further we push aloneness away, the less are we able to cope with it, and the more terrifying it gets. Some philosophers believe that loneliness is the only true feeling there is. We live orphaned on a tiny rock in the immense vastness of space, with no hint of even the simplest form of life anywhere around us for billions upon billions of miles, alone beyond all imagining. We live locked in our own heads and can never entirely know the experience of another person. Even if we're surrounded by family and friends, we journey into death completely alone.

"Solitude is the profoundest fact of the human condition," wrote the Mexican poet and Nobel laureate Octavio Paz. "Ultimately, and precisely in the deepest and most important matters, we are unspeakably alone," wrote the Austro-German poet Rainer Maria Rilke.

Surprisingly, I receive one final letter from Knight. It's an elegy to our relationship, five lines long. He instructs me to purchase some flowers for my wife, and candy for the cowboys, "for compensation of your absence to Maine." Then he tells me never to come back. "For now and then hence."

He doesn't sign his name, of course, but for the first time, he includes a small doodle, done with colored pencils. It's a flower, just a single flower, a daisy with red petals and a yellow center and two green leaves, blooming at the bottom of his note. An unmistakably optimistic sign. I take it as a signal that he's adapted at least somewhat to his new life. I take it to mean that even if he can never live the way he wishes to, he won't be walking with the Lady of the Woods. I take it as a sign of hope.

Sometimes, though, I can't help but wonder, What if? What if Sergeant Hughes hadn't been so dedicated, and Knight had never been caught? Knight told me that he planned to stay out there forever. He was willing to die in his camp, the spot where he was most content. Even without a cleanup crew, it would not take too long for nature to reclaim the area, ferns sprouting, roots creeping through, his tent and his body and eventually his propane cylinders consumed by the soil.

It's the ending, I believe, that Knight planned. He wasn't going to leave behind a single recorded thought, not a photo, not an idea. No person would know of his experience. Nothing would ever be written about him. He would simply vanish, and no one on this teeming planet would notice. His end wouldn't create so much as a ripple on North Pond. It would have been an existence, a life, of utter perfection.

Gratitude

For patience and understanding and love:

Jill Barker Finkel	Phoebe Finkel
Beckett Finkel	Alix Finkel

For responding with elegance and intelligence:

Christopher Knight

For tinkering with the parts:

Andrew Miller	Stuart Krichevsky
Michael Benoist	Jim Nelson
Geoffrey Gagnon	Paul Prince
Riley Blanton	Max Thorn
Robin Desser	Sonny Mehta
Paul Bogaards	Jeanne Harper
Rachel Elson	Adam Cohen
Diana Finkel	Ben Woodbeck
Paul Finkel	Mark Miller
Janet Markman	Shana Cohen
Mike Sottak	Ross Harris
Emma Dries	David Gore
Bonnie Thompson	Maria Massey

Gratitude

For insight into Knight:

Matt Hongoltz-Hetling	Terry Hughes	Diane Vance
Harvey Chesley	Andrew Vietze	Jennifer Smith-Mayo
Simon Baron-Cohen	Catherine Benoist	Peter Deri
Stephen M. Edelson	Thomas W. Frazier	Jill Hooley
Roger Bellavance	Tony Bellavance	Stephen M. Prescott
Tom Sturtevant	Neal Patterson	Martha Patterson
Pete Cogswell	Lillie Cogswell	Jodie Mosher-Towle
Gerard Spence	Catherine Lord	Carroll Bubar
David Proulx	Louise Proulx	John Cazell
Greg Hollands	Garry Hollands	Brenda Hollands
Debbie Baker	Donna Bolduc	T. J. Bolduc
Maeghan Maloney	Walter McKee	Robert Kull
Fred King	Larry Gaspar	Mary Hinkley
Michael Parker	Rick Watson	Wayne Jewell
Bruce Hillman	Kyle McDougle	Carol Sullivan
Lauren Brent	Kerry Vigue	Kevin Trask
Larry Stewart	Jeff Young	Phil Dow
John Catanzarite	Kevin Wilson	Ryan Reardon
Michael Seamans	Rachel Ohm	Bob Milliken
John Boivin	Amanda Dow	Monica Brand
Lena Friedrich	Meng-hu	Angela Minnick
Catherine Lovendahl	Jim Cormier	Debbie Wright Theriault

For friendship, encouragement, and one last drink:

Dada Morabia	Gabrielle Morabia	Bill Magill
Ian Taylor	Laurence Schofield	Barbara Strauss
Toni Sottak	Larry Smith	Piper Kerman
Jill Cowdry	Lawrence Weschler	Abby Ellin
HJ Schmidt	Martyn Scott	Joshua Willcocks
Randall Lane	Michel Pfister	Emmanuelle Hartmann
Tim Hartmann	Max Reichel	Gary Parker
Tilly Parker	John Byorth	Alan Schwarz

Theresa Barker	Harris Barker	Brett Cline
Arron Bradshaw Cline	Brian Whitlock	Arthur Goldfrank
Tara Goldfrank	Eddie Steinhauer	Pascale Hickman
Mohamed El-Bouarfaoui	Naima El-Bouarfaoui	Adi Bukman
Jake Werner	Carma Miller	Jim Schipf
Annette Schipf	Michaela Struss	Ben Struss
Chris Anderson	Marion Durand	Kent Davis
David Hirshey	Ryan West	Patty West

A Note on the Reporting

The Kennebec County Correctional Facility permits a maximum of two meetings per week with an inmate, each lasting one hour. I visited Christopher Knight twice in the last week of August 2013—this was after he'd written me five letters—and then twice more in September, and a further two times in early October. In late October, I attended Knight's court hearing and visited him three times. Knight himself is obviously the chief source of material for this book.

Knight was never thrilled to see me, but for each of our nine jail visits, we conversed the entire time, through old-fashioned phone receivers. After an hour, the phones automatically cut off, but by the second visit, Knight had learned, from observing another inmate, a jail trick. If a guard hadn't arrived to unlock Knight's side of the visiting booth, he fiddled with the hook switch on the phone's cradle—I imagined the maneuver was like one of Knight's lock-breaking moves—and was able to reconnect the lines, allowing us to chat for a few extra minutes.

So despite Knight's reticence and his lack of joy at seeing me, he wanted to continue talking for as long as possible.

After his release, during our intense visit on his property, he referred to me as his "Boswell"—a reference to James Boswell, the eighteenth-century Scottish writer best known for *The Life of Samuel Johnson,* one of the more famous biographies in all of literature.

The Life of Samuel Johnson is immense—more than a thousand pages in most editions—and I told Knight that my book would likely be far shorter. Knight seemed disappointed to hear this. "I like long books better," he told me.

I made a total of seven reporting trips to Maine over the course of two years, the final one in April 2015. I also wrote a magazine story about Knight, which was published in the September 2014 issue of *GQ* magazine. The *GQ* story was fact-checked by a professional fact-checker named Riley Blanton, and Blanton, along with another professional fact-checker, Max Thorn, took on the task of confirming all of the material in this book. I did not change any names in this account, nor did I alter any identifying details. No one interviewed was granted any editorial control.

Every trip to Maine, I spent a couple of days driving the dirt roads of North and Little North Ponds, often visiting house after house, like a door-to-door peddler. I spoke with at least forty families who own a cabin or permanent home in the area. The majority of cabin owners are native Mainers, most of the rest come from the Boston area, and a few families live farther afield. Whether or not a particular family liked or detested Knight—some families were deeply split—I was warmly welcomed. At several places, I was invited to stay for dinner, or drink beers on the porch, or come along on a canoe ride. Everyone, it seemed, wanted to tell their version of the hermit story.

David and Louise Proulx, whose tiny black-and-white television had been stolen by Knight, suffered at least fifty break-ins over the decades, and they described the strange psychological effects of the crimes—at first, they were convinced it was one of their own children who was guilty; then they seriously wondered if they had begun to lose their minds. Pete Cogswell, whose size thirty-eight Lands' End jeans and brown leather belt were stolen, and his wife, Lillie Cogswell, who worked in the Texas criminal justice system for more than thirty years, spoke with me at length, describing the details of Knight's confounding break-ins and speculating on what might be an appropriate punishment for him. Donna and T. J. Bolduc shared with me their game-camera photos of Knight, as well as their Skinnygirl margarita mix joke.

Garry Hollands, one of the first people to hang a bag on his cabin's door with offerings for the hermit, spoke of all the books he'd lost, and how he'd balanced a nearly invisible bit of fishing line over his door that would be dislodged when someone opened it, so he could tell when he'd been burglarized. Debbie Baker described how fearful her young children were of the hermit—it was her family that nicknamed him the Hungry Man. Neal Patterson recounted his fourteen nights waiting in his cabin in the dark, with a gun, trying to catch the hermit.

Sergeant Terry Hughes spent hours telling me about his hermit obsession, and one evening he took me around in his pickup truck to check his traps, then brought me to his clubhouse and provided instructions as I skinned my first-ever muskrat. State Trooper Diane Vance met me after Knight's court hearing and spoke with me several times over the phone. Both the district attorney, Maeghan Maloney, and Knight's attorney, Walter McKee, granted me interviews. No one in Knight's family spoke with me, but dozens of people in the Albion community did, including several of Knight's former teachers and classmates, as well as a few longtime friends of the Knight family.

During each trip to Maine, I visited Knight's camp. It was never easy to find. There is no way to overstate how thick and confusing the Jarsey is, or the astonishment provoked, every time, by stepping from the dense forest into the site.

To attempt to comprehend more of Knight's mind-set, I had lengthy telephone conversations and e-mail chats with several psychologists and autism experts, including Simon Baron-Cohen of Cambridge University; Catherine Benoist, who runs a clinical practice near Chicago; Peter Deri, in private practice in New York; Stephen M. Edelson of the Autism Research Institute, in San Diego; Thomas W. Frazier of the Center for Autism at the Cleveland Clinic; Jill Hooley of Harvard University; and Catherine Lord of Weill Cornell Medicine. Stephen M. Prescott, president of the Oklahoma Medical Research Foundation, spoke with me about the nature of communicable diseases and how it was possible that Knight had never gotten sick.

In order to gain insight into the ordeals of forced isolation, I corresponded extensively with John Catanzarite, an inmate in the California prison system who spent almost fourteen years locked in solitary confinement. I also read a dozen other accounts from solitary prisoners.

There's an ocean of hermit literature; I began my reading on one shore, with Lao-tzu's *Tao Te Ching* (I recommend the Red Pine translation), and started swimming from there. Excellent explorations of the history and motivations of hermits include *Solitude* by Anthony Storr, *A Pelican in the Wilderness* by Isabel Colegate, *Hermits* by Peter France, and *Solitude* by Philip Koch.

Perceptive and valuable personal explorations of time alone include *A Book of Silence* by Sara Maitland, *Party of One* by Anneli Rufus, *Migrations to Solitude* by Sue Halpern, *Journal of a Solitude* by May Sarton, *The Point of Vanishing* by Howard Axelrod, *Solitude* by Robert Kull, *Pilgrim at Tinker Creek* by Annie Dillard, *The Diving Bell and the Butterfly* by Jean-Dominique Bauby, *A Field Guide to Getting Lost* by Rebecca Solnit, *The Story of My Heart* by Richard Jefferies, *Thoughts in Solitude* by Thomas Merton, and the incomparable *Walden* by Henry David Thoreau.

Adventure tales offering superb insight into solitude, both its horror and its beauty, include *The Long Way* by Bernard Moitessier, *The Strange Last Voyage of Donald Crowhurst* by Nicholas Tomalin and Ron Hall, *A Voyage for Madmen* by Peter Nichols, *Into the Wild* by Jon Krakauer, and *Alone* by Richard E. Byrd.

Science-focused books that provided me with further understanding of how solitude affects people include *Social* by Matthew D. Lieberman, *Loneliness* by John T. Cacioppo and William Patrick, *Quiet* by Susan Cain, *Neurotribes* by

Steve Silberman, and *An Anthropologist on Mars* by Oliver Sacks.

Also offering astute ideas about aloneness are *Cave in the Snow* by Vicki Mackenzie, *The Life of Saint Anthony* by Saint Athanasius, *Letters to a Young Poet* by Rainer Maria Rilke, the essays of Ralph Waldo Emerson (especially "Nature" and "Self-Reliance") and Friedrich Nietzsche (especially "Man Alone with Himself"), the verse of William Wordsworth, and the poems of Han-shan, Shih-te, and Wang Fan-chih.

It was essential for me to read two of Knight's favorite books: *Notes from the Underground* by Fyodor Dostoyevsky and *Very Special People* by Frederick Drimmer. This book's epigraph, attributed to Socrates, comes from the C. D. Yonge translation of Diogenes Laërtius's third-century A.D. work *The Lives and Opinions of Eminent Philosophers.*

The Hermitary website, which offers hundreds of articles on every aspect of hermit life, is an invaluable resource— I spent weeks immersed in the site, though I did not qualify to become a member of the hermit-only chat groups.

My longtime researcher, Jeanne Harper, dug up hundreds of reports on hermits and loners throughout history. I was fascinated by the stories of Japanese soldiers who continued fighting World War II for decades on remote Pacific islands, though none seemed to be completely alone for more than a few years at a time. Still, Hiroo Onoda's *No Surrender* is a fascinating account.

And then there's the story of the last survivor of an Amazon tribe. In 2007, after several failed attempts to make peaceful contact with this man, who once fired an arrow into the chest of a rescue worker, the Brazilian government provided him with a thirty-one-square-mile region of rain forest. The land is off-limits to everyone except this man. He traps animals for food. He has been completely alone for about twenty years. Now that Chris Knight resides in society, this man, whose name is unknown—as is the name of his tribe and the language he speaks—may be the most isolated person in the world.

A Note About the Author

Michael Finkel is the author of *True Story: Murder, Memoir, Mea Culpa,* which was adapted into a 2015 motion picture. He has reported from more than fifty countries and written for *National Geographic, GQ, Rolling Stone, Esquire, Vanity Fair, The Atlantic,* and *The New York Times Magazine.* He lives in western Montana.

A Note on the Type

This book was set in Granjon, a type named in compliment to Robert Granjon, a type cutter and printer active from 1523 to 1590. Granjon was designed by George W. Jones, who based his drawings on a face used by Claude Garamond (ca. 1480–1561). Granjon more closely resembles Garamond's own type than do any of the various modern faces that bear his name.

Composed by North Market Street Graphics
Lancaster, Pennsylvania

Printed and bound by Berryville Graphics
Berryville, Virginia

Designed by M. Kristen Bearse